BIG
SCIENCE
ACTIVITY BOOK

Buster Books

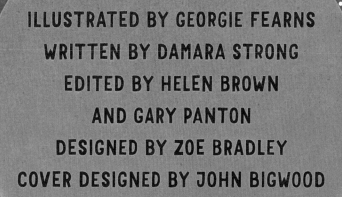

ILLUSTRATED BY GEORGIE FEARNS
WRITTEN BY DAMARA STRONG
EDITED BY HELEN BROWN
AND GARY PANTON
DESIGNED BY ZOE BRADLEY
COVER DESIGNED BY JOHN BIGWOOD

First published in Great Britain in 2021 by Buster Books, an imprint of
Michael O'Mara Books Limited, 9 Lion Yard, Tremadoc Road, London SW4 7NQ

 www.mombooks.com/buster   Buster Books   @BusterBooks   @buster_books

ISBN: 978-1-78055-694-9

1 3 5 7 9 10 8 6 4 2

This book was printed in March 2021 by Leo Paper Products Ltd,
Heshan Astros Printing Limited, Xuantan Temple Industrial Zone,
Gulao Town, Heshan City, Guangdong Province, China.

STEP INTO THE PUZZLE LAB

Science is all around you. From the stars in the night sky, to the fish in the sea, to the blood flowing through your own body, it's all a part of what makes science incredible.

Inside this book are over 100 awesome activities all about how science shapes the world. Along the way, you can discover loads of fascinating facts all about great scientists, science history and how things work. Whether you're already a big science fan or you're just starting out on your science journey, you're bound to find plenty to fill you with wonder.

If you get stuck on any of the tougher puzzles, don't worry. You can find all the answers at the back of the book, on pages 116–127. There's also a glossary on page 128, to help you out with any science words you might not know.

Now, pull on your lab coat and get ready to become a puzzle professor.

COUNTING IN THE LAB

These scientists are busy in their laboratory. How many of the objects in the checklist can you spot in the scene? Add up your answers, then check your total matches the one shown.

CHECKLIST

CONICAL FLASK

BUNSEN BURNER

TEST TUBE

SAFETY GOGGLES

GLOVE

PETRI DISH

TOTAL = 43

The Bunsen burner is named after its inventor, Doctor Robert Bunsen. Doctor Bunsen also co-discovered the elements caesium (Cs) and rubidium (Rb), adding them to the periodic table.

During World War II, engineer Percy Spencer was testing military radar technology when he noticed that the chocolate bar in his pocket had melted. This led to the invention of microwave ovens.

In 1928, a biologist called Alexander Fleming found a dish that had been left uncovered. A blue-green mould had formed, which killed off all surrounding bacteria. The mould contained a powerful 'antibiotic', now known as penicillin. Antibiotics are medicines that search out and destroy the bacteria that can make you sick.

TURNING TURBINE

Steam can be used to create electricity. Take the steam through the factory maze to the turbine, then pick any route along the power cables to reach the house.

In a power plant, steam makes wheels spin in a turbine, producing 'rotational energy' which is used to generate electricity. The electricity then travels along cables to people's homes, giving power to electronic devices.

STEAM

START

TURBINE

FINISH

Electricity travels at the speed of light. That's more than 300,000 km per second! How quickly can you solve the maze?

ACID OR ALKALI?

The pH scale is used to measure whether a substance is an acid or an alkali. The more acidic a substance, the lower it goes on the pH scale (towards 1). The more alkaline, the higher it is on the pH scale (towards 14). Read the descriptions below and then place the items on the dotted lines on the pH scale.

The acidity of a substance is determined by its number of hydrogen ions. This is its 'power of hydrogen', or pH.

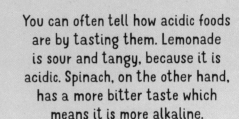

You can often tell how acidic foods are by tasting them. Lemonade is sour and tangy, because it is acidic. Spinach, on the other hand, has a more bitter taste which means it is more alkaline.

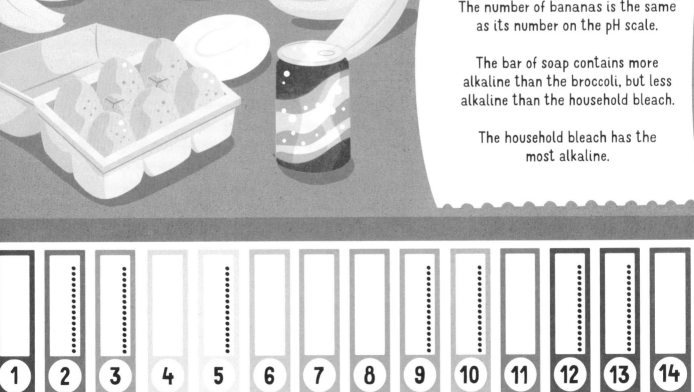

The number of lemons is the same as its number on the pH scale.

The can of soda contains more acid than the bananas, but less acid than the lemons.

The eggs contain more alkaline than the bananas, but less alkaline than the broccoli.

The number of bananas is the same as its number on the pH scale.

The bar of soap contains more alkaline than the broccoli, but less alkaline than the household bleach.

The household bleach has the most alkaline.

| 1 | 2 | 3 | 4 | 5 | 6 | 7 | 8 | 9 | 10 | 11 | 12 | 13 | 14 |

ACID   **NEUTRAL**   **ALKALI**

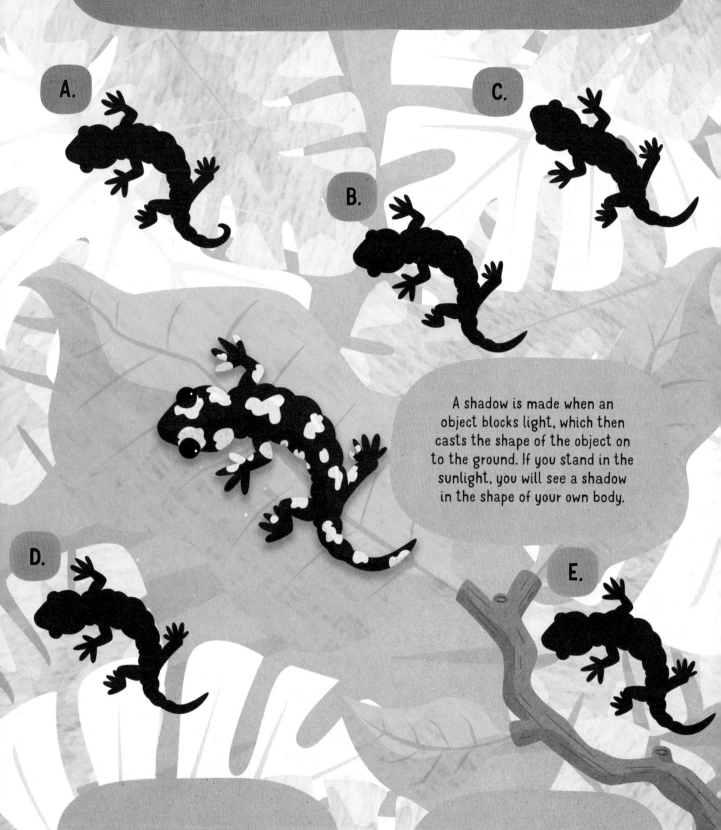

SALAMANDER SHADOW
Which shadow matches the shape of the salamander on the leaf?

A.

C.

B.

A shadow is made when an object blocks light, which then casts the shape of the object on to the ground. If you stand in the sunlight, you will see a shadow in the shape of your own body.

D.

E.

When your part of the Earth turns away from the Sun, the planet blocks the light from reaching you, putting you in shadow and causing darkness.

Shadows create cooler temperatures. In the hot summer, the shadow from a building or tree can often be a place to cool off and get out of the Sun.

TASTE-BUD TRAIL

Follow the food in the order shown on the wooden platter from start to finish. You can move across, up and down but not diagonally.

START

FINISH

Your taste buds are on the upper surface of your tongue. They help you tell the difference between five different tastes – bitter, sweet, sour, salty and savoury.

Your senses are made up of cells that send signals to your brain. Your five senses are smell, taste, touch, hearing and sight.

MAGNETIC MAYHEM

If something is 'magnetic', it is metal and will be drawn to a magnet. Circle the items below that are magnetic.

When two magnets are close, they create pushing or pulling forces on one another. These forces are strongest at the ends of the magnets. The two ends of a magnet are known as its 'north pole' and 'south pole'.

If you put two magnets together with the same poles pointing towards one another, the magnets will push away from each other. However, if you put two magnets together with different poles pointing towards one another, the magnets will pull towards each other.

10

URINE UNCERTAINTY

Urine, or wee, can be used in different ways. Read the statements below and see if you can work out which are true and which are false. Don't try any of these at home!

Sniffing urine can help if you have a blocked nose.

Dogs use their wee to mark their territory.

Drinking urine can help to maintain a healthy heart.

Urine in the soil can help plants grow.

Urine has been used to make gunpowder.

The Romans used urine to whiten their teeth.

CRYSTAL CAVE JIGSAW

Which of the tiles below are from the crystal cave scene on the right-hand page?

Heat, pressure and fluid build up over billions of years to form pure minerals, which take the form of crystals. Some of the largest crystals on Earth are in Mexico's Cave of Crystals, where huge crystal pillars stretch up to 11 metres in length.

A.

C.

Around 26 million years ago, the Cave of Crystals sat beneath a volcanic field and was filled with a boiling hot fluid called 'anhydrite'. When the fluid cooled, it created the cave's giant crystals.

B.

D.

E.

F.

Scientists recently found 50,000-year-old microscopic life trapped inside the Cave of Crystals' pillars. The tiny microbes thrive on the iron, sulphur and other elements found in the crystals.

MOMENTUM SEQUENCES

Which number is missing from each of the following sequences?

4 8 12 16 ....

Momentum is determined by a combination of 'mass' and 'velocity'. Mass is the amount of atoms in an object, while velocity describes how fast an object is going and which direction it is moving in.

10 16 22 28 ....

Sir Isaac Newton's second law of physics describes how an object's momentum changes in different scenarios. For example, if you throw a ball into the wind, it won't travel as far as if there is no wind.

.... 5 7 10 14

FLOWER POWER

Plants need water to absorb nutrients from the soil. Can you find the correct route from the watering can to the soil below?

START

Plants are very important to both people and animals. They can provide oxygen, food, shelter, medicine and even fuel.

Water and nutrients travel through the roots and stem to the leaves. The leaves take in sunlight and carbon dioxide, and produce food for the plant. This process is called 'photosynthesis'.

FINISH

RESISTANCE REVEAL

Join up the dots to complete this picture. What is revealed?

Gravity pulls air downwards to create 'atmospheric pressure' (also known as air pressure), which is the weight of the air on the surface of the Earth.

A person falling from a plane will fall at about 200 km per hour. With a canopy like the one in the picture, they'll slow right down to around 20 km per hour.

In the picture, air pressure is increasing below the canopy. This is decreasing the person's momentum so that they fall more slowly and can land safely.

LABORATORY SUDOKU

Fill in the two sudoku grids with these test tubes and flasks commonly found in laboratories. Each row, column and six-square block must only contain one of each type.

EXAMPLE:

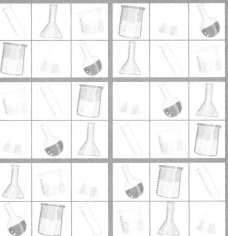

In the 1800s, Louis Pasteur sterilized a liquid in two flasks. One flask had a long stem to prevent anything from entering, and the other had a broken stem exposing the liquid to air. The flask with the long stem remained sterile, while the liquid exposed to air became full of bacteria. This proved that life does not simply appear from non-living things, as people once thought.

1.

2.

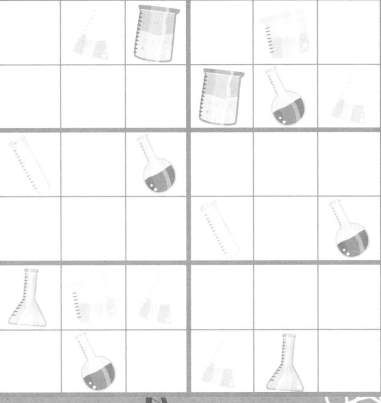

WIND TURBINE SPOT THE DIFFERENCE

Can you spot ten differences between
these two wind-turbine scenes?

Most wind power comes from wind
spinning the blades of turbines. This
creates 'rotational energy', which can
be used to produce electricity.

Unlike fossil fuels, wind turbines
do not cause any environmentally
harmful pollution.

SPACE QUIZ

Put your cosmic knowledge to the test.

1. What is the Sun mainly made from?
   a. Gas b. Liquid lava c. Molten iron

2. Which of these planets is the smallest?
   a. Uranus b. Mercury c. Earth

3. What are comets mostly made of?
   a. Ice, dust and rock b. Rusty metal c. Hot, liquid rock

4. How many moons does Mars have?
   a. 13 b. 50 c. 2

5. What is the closest planet to the Sun?
   a. Neptune b. Mercury c. Earth

6. The largest volcano in the Solar System is called Olympus Mons. Where is it?
   a. Jupiter b. Venus c. Mars

7. Where is the asteroid belt?
   a. Between Earth and Venus b. Between Earth and Mars
   c. Between Mars and Jupiter

8. What planet has the nickname 'Red Planet'?
   a. Mars b. Mercury c. Venus

9. Which of these planets is the hottest?
   a. Jupiter b. Neptune c. Venus

10. Which planet do the moons Oberon and Titania belong to?
    a. Venus b. Uranus c. Jupiter

CROSSED WIRES

Follow the wires to work out which switch
is charging which mobile phone.

1.

2.

3.

4.

5.

6.

Electric charges can be
positive or negative. When
the negative charges (or
electrons) build up they give
us electricity, which can
then give power to objects or
devices. If your lights are on,
you have electrons to thank!

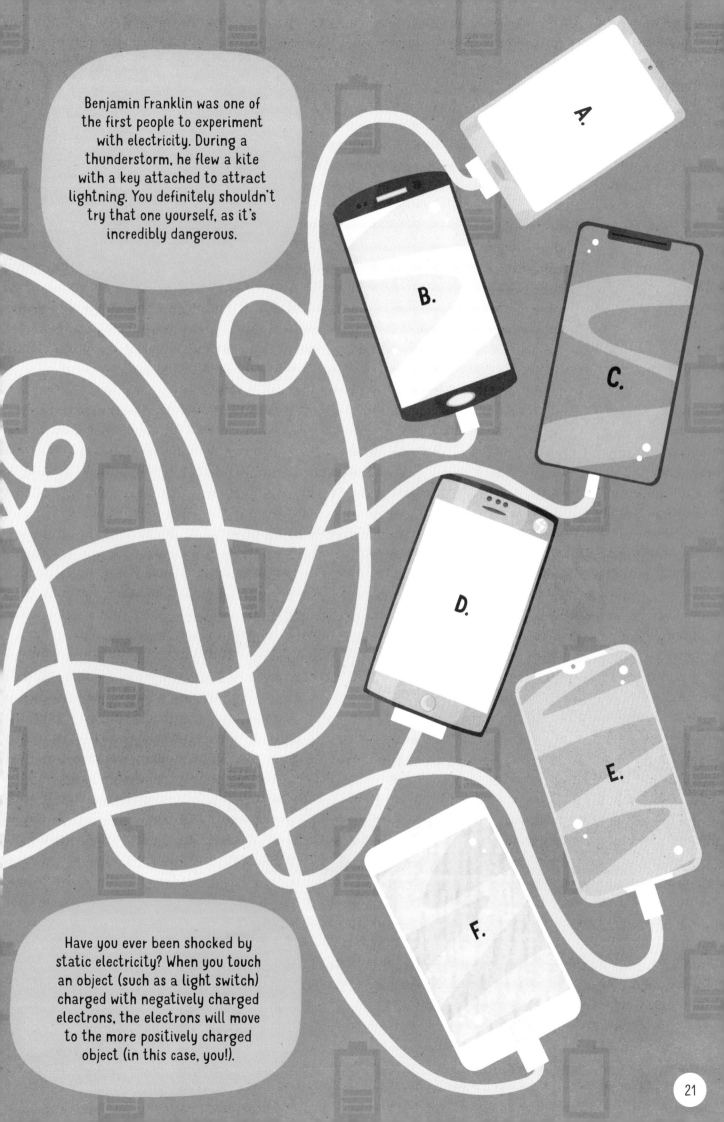

Benjamin Franklin was one of the first people to experiment with electricity. During a thunderstorm, he flew a kite with a key attached to attract lightning. You definitely shouldn't try that one yourself, as it's incredibly dangerous.

A.

B.

C.

D.

E.

F.

Have you ever been shocked by static electricity? When you touch an object (such as a light switch) charged with negatively charged electrons, the electrons will move to the more positively charged object (in this case, you!).

SEASON SECTIONS

Can you divide the page into four separate sections, using just three straight lines? Each section must contain a snowman, a sledge, a tree and a frozen lake.

Snow forms when the temperature of the air is at or below 0°C (32°F). It can be too warm to snow, but as long as there is moisture in the air it can never be too cold to snow.

Most heavy snowfall happens when the temperature near the ground is -9°C (16°F) or warmer, since warmer air can hold more moisture. The coldest temperature ever recorded on Earth is -89.2°C (-128.6°F) in Antarctica.

MICROSCOPE PARTS

Circle the group below that contains all of the
parts that you need to make this microscope.

A.

B.

Magnification has been known about for a long time. In 1267, the philosopher Roger Bacon wrote about the idea of being able to count dust particles if they could be seen more closely.

Father-son team Hans and Zacharias Janssen invented the compound microscope in the 16th century. By putting lenses on opposite ends of a tube, they were able to make objects appear up to nine times larger. Today's versions can magnify by up to 2,000 times.

C.

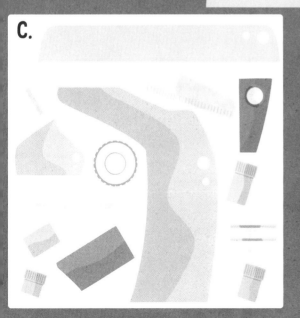

D.

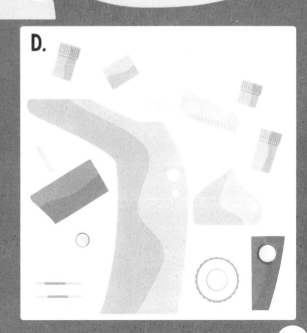

AMAZING LIFE CYCLES

All living things go through life cycles. Animals produce offspring and plants produce seeds which become new plants. Go along the rows and choose the correct options from the bottom of the page to complete these life cycles.

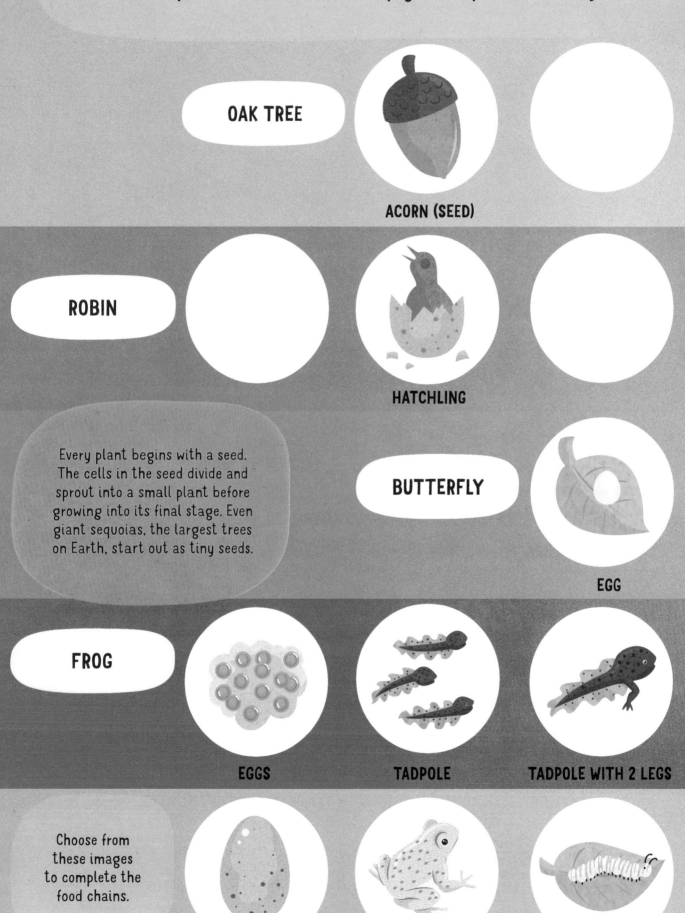

OAK TREE

ACORN (SEED)

ROBIN

HATCHLING

Every plant begins with a seed. The cells in the seed divide and sprout into a small plant before growing into its final stage. Even giant sequoias, the largest trees on Earth, start out as tiny seeds.

BUTTERFLY

EGG

FROG

EGGS

TADPOLE

TADPOLE WITH 2 LEGS

Choose from these images to complete the food chains.

EGG

ADULT FROG

CATERPILLAR

Some animals go through an extreme life cycle change called a 'metamorphosis'. For example, a sea urchin starts as a small larva with a tiny bud. This bud turns into the adult, while the rest of its body disappears.

SAPLING

MATURE OAK TREE

FLEDGLING

JUVENILE

ADULT ROBIN

ADULT BUTTERFLY

TADPOLE WITH 4 LEGS

FROGLET (YOUNG FROG)

NESTLING

CHRYSALIS

SEEDLING

FORCES IN ACTION

Everything on Earth is powered by forces. When you move down a slide, gravity pulls you downwards, while friction works against gravity to slow you down. Solve the sums on the slides to work out the speed of each child.

A.

7 SECONDS

+ 16 SECONDS

+ 20 SECONDS

- 9 SECONDS

X 2 SECONDS

- 19 SECONDS

B.

8 SECONDS

- 1 SECOND

+ 5 SECONDS

X 2 SECONDS

- 7 SECONDS

- 6 SECONDS

C.

9 SECONDS

- 3 SECONDS

+ 11 SECONDS

- 4 SECONDS

+ 2 SECONDS

- 12 SECONDS

A 'force' is a push or pull on an object. Examples of forces include the wind pushing a sailboat through the water and a person kicking a ball.

'Friction' is a force that slows down one object moving over another object, such as a surface. The smoother a surface is, the less friction it creates, and the faster the object can go.

COMBUSTION COUNTING

Count how many of each firework you can spot from the checklist below, then add up your answers. Check your total matches the one shown.

CHECKLIST

RING

CHRYSANTHEMUM

CRACKLE

WHIRLWIND

WAVE

GLITTER

TOTAL = 20

Did you know that each firework colour is composed of different chemicals? Blue fireworks are a mixture of copper and chloride, while yellow fireworks are composed of sodium and chloride (just like your table salt).

THE HEAT IS ON

Can you fill the thermometers with the correct amount of liquid? The numbers indicate how many squares in each row and column contain liquid. Liquid always starts filling from the round part at the bottom of a thermometer, and not every thermometer has to contain liquid.

EXAMPLE:

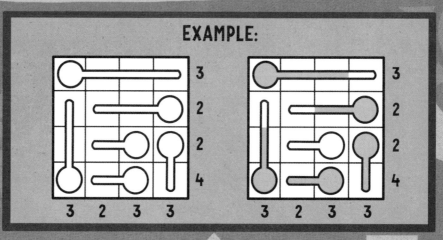

The first attempt at measuring temperature was in 170 CE when a Greek scientist called Galen mixed equal amounts of boiling water with ice. He called the result 'neutral temperature'.

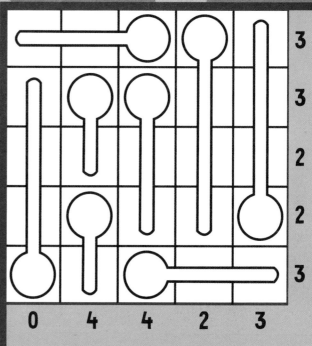

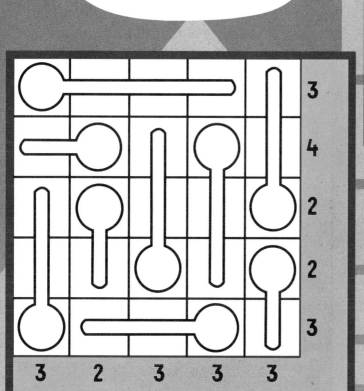

Fahrenheit, Celsius and Kelvin are the three main temperature scales used today. While Fahrenheit is standard in the United States, most of the rest of the world uses Celsius. Kelvin is mainly used in scientific research.

MATERIAL MATCH UP

Match up each object from the pencil case
with the material from which it is made.

WOOD

PLASTIC

GLASS

METAL

RUBBER

PAPER

You come into contact with lots
of different materials every day.
The materials used to create
objects are chosen based on
many factors, including strength,
ability to move electrical
currents, resistance to heat
and much more.

Think of the story of *The Three
Little Pigs*. Materials matter! Each
type of material has a different
strength or weakness. For example,
the wolf couldn't blow down the pigs'
brick house, but blew down their
straw house with ease.

PUMP THE BLOOD

Complete these two mazes in the heart to help pump blood around the body. Start on the right side of the heart to pump deoxygenated blood to the lungs and then move on to the left side to pump oxygenated blood to the body's other organs.

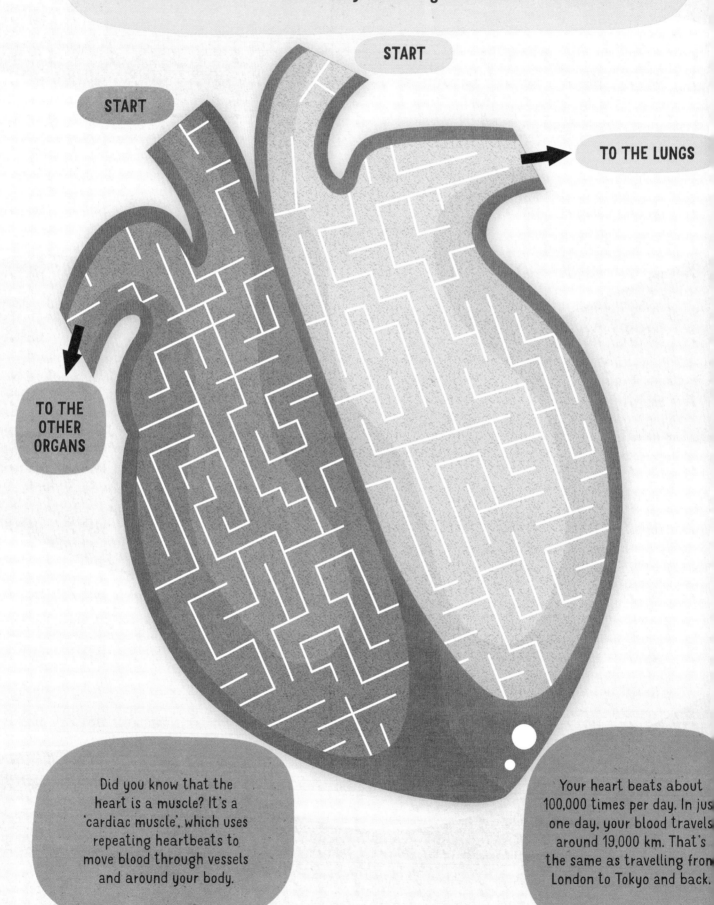

START

START

TO THE LUNGS

TO THE OTHER ORGANS

Did you know that the heart is a muscle? It's a 'cardiac muscle', which uses repeating heartbeats to move blood through vessels and around your body.

Your heart beats about 100,000 times per day. In jus one day, your blood travels around 19,000 km. That's the same as travelling from London to Tokyo and back.

ATOMS ADDITION

These four atomic structures each contain a maths problem. Add up the numbers in the electrons and write the total in the nucleus. Which one has the highest number of electrons?

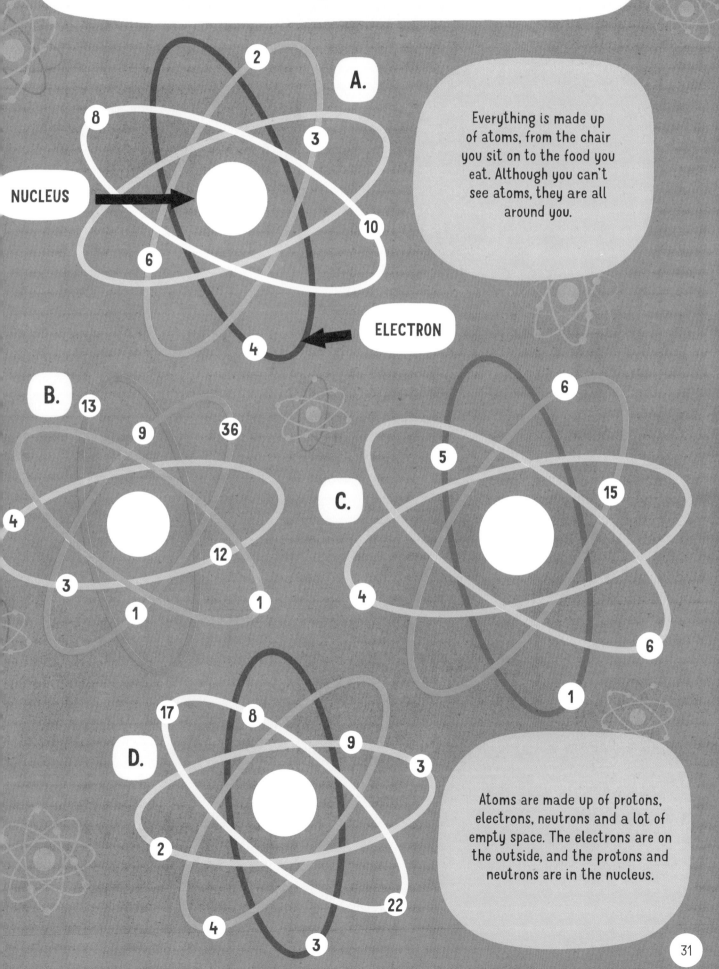

A.

NUCLEUS

ELECTRON

Everything is made up of atoms, from the chair you sit on to the food you eat. Although you can't see atoms, they are all around you.

B.

C.

D.

Atoms are made up of protons, electrons, neutrons and a lot of empty space. The electrons are on the outside, and the protons and neutrons are in the nucleus.

DATA DILEMMA

A scientist is conducting an experiment on how long it takes for apples to turn mouldy. They have written a report and plotted their results on a bar graph. Read their notes and work out which bar graph is showing the correct results.

EQUIPMENT

- 1 apple cut into 4 equal pieces
- 4 jars
- Vinegar
- Salt water (1 tablespoon salt dissolved in hot water)
- Lemon juice

METHOD

1. Put an apple piece in each jar.

2. Fill the first three jars halfway with one of the liquids. Make sure the apple piece is covered by the liquid. The fourth apple and jar is the 'control group', so shouldn't have any liquid added to it. This will show what happens to the apple when it is kept in the same conditions as the other pieces, but is not tampered with.

3. Keep the jars in a cool area for a week and observe the changes.

RESULTS

On the second day, the apple piece in the lemon juice started to go mouldy. This could be because the micro-organisms flourished in the sugary environment.

The next apple piece to go mouldy was the control group. It shrivelled up, but there was only a little bit of mould.

The apple piece in the vinegar went mouldy on day five. This mould took a longer time to form because vinegar has anti-microbial properties.

The apple piece in the salt water remained fresh for the longest. This is because salt is a natural preservative.

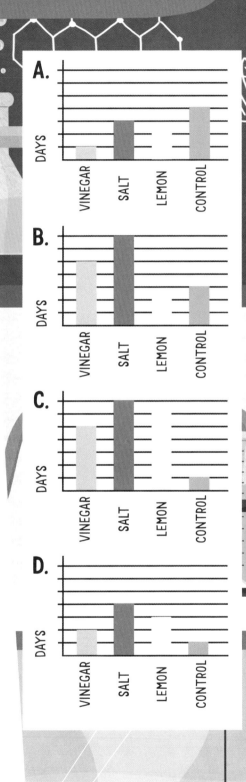

WHAT A PONG!

Can you follow the tangled lines to match the noses to the smelly food?

A.
B.
C.
D.
E.
F.

1.
2.
3.
4.
5.
6.

Different smells can change your mood or trigger a memory. They can even keep you safe from harm. If something smells like it has gone off, you know not to eat it, which helps to keep you healthy.

Take a deep breath. Can you smell anything? You probably aren't smelling exactly the same smells as the person next to you, as the cells in noses vary from person to person.

OUT OF THIS WORLD

Use the clues to work out which planet is which.

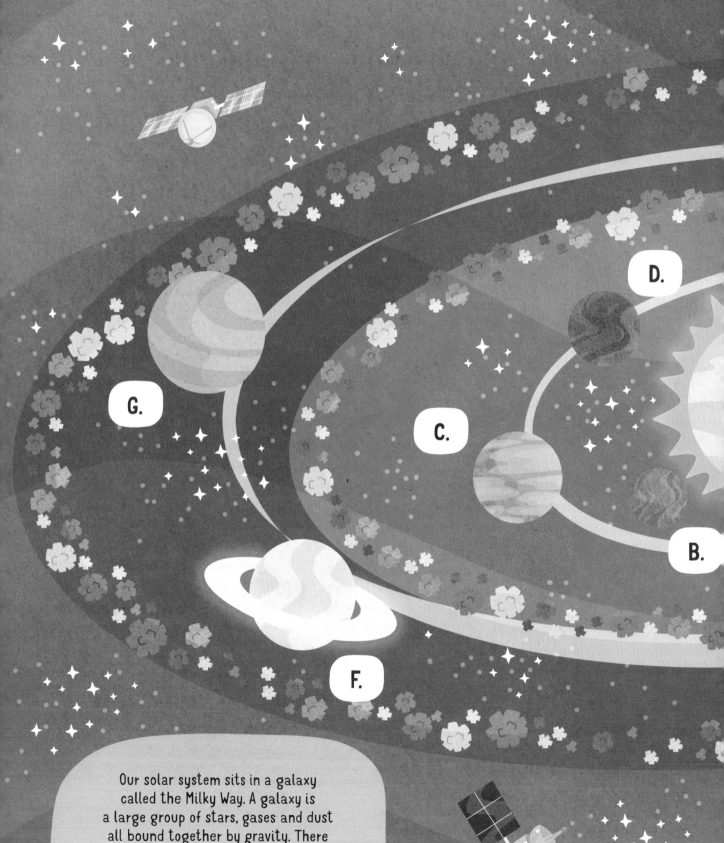

Our solar system sits in a galaxy called the Milky Way. A galaxy is a large group of stars, gases and dust all bound together by gravity. There are around 100 billion stars in the Milky Way, but our solar system has just one of them – the Sun!

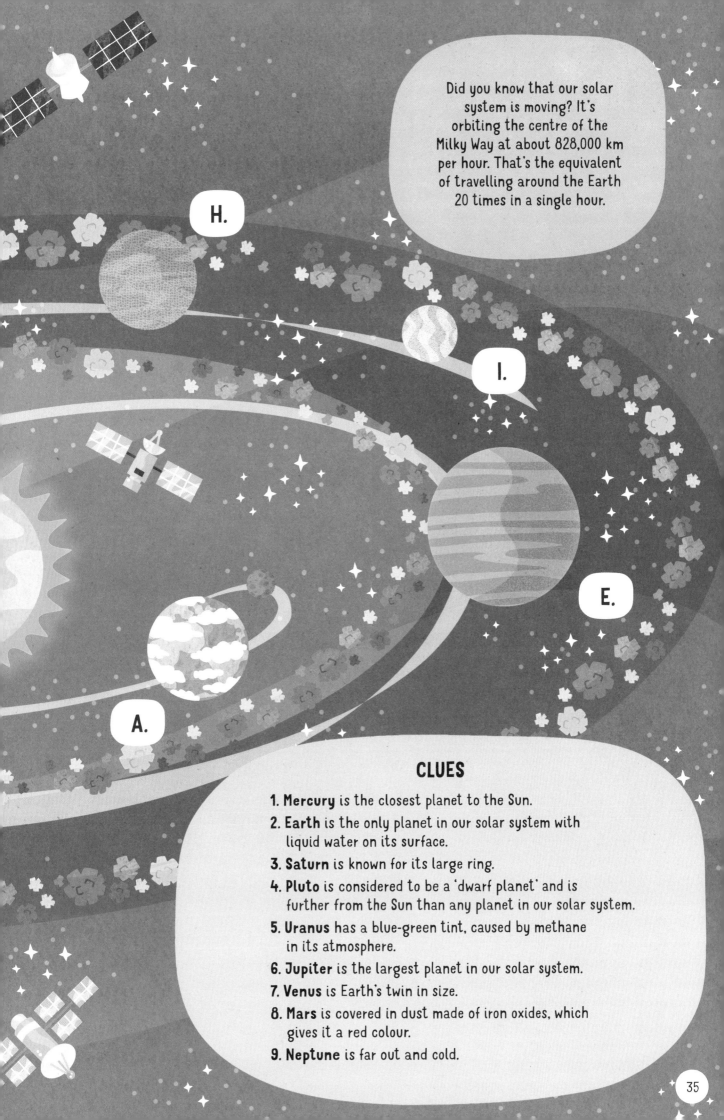

CLUES

1. **Mercury** is the closest planet to the Sun.
2. **Earth** is the only planet in our solar system with liquid water on its surface.
3. **Saturn** is known for its large ring.
4. **Pluto** is considered to be a 'dwarf planet' and is further from the Sun than any planet in our solar system.
5. **Uranus** has a blue-green tint, caused by methane in its atmosphere.
6. **Jupiter** is the largest planet in our solar system.
7. **Venus** is Earth's twin in size.
8. **Mars** is covered in dust made of iron oxides, which gives it a red colour.
9. **Neptune** is far out and cold.

HORSE AND FOAL JIGSAW

Which of the tiles below is not from the
picture of a horse and its foal?

Baby animals have all
sorts of different names.
Baby porcupines are called
'porcupettes', baby fish are
called 'fry' and baby elephant
seals are called 'weaners'.

A.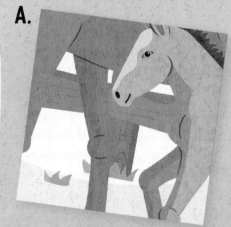

B.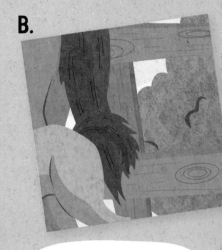

C.

D.

Some animal babies stay
with their mothers for years,
while others don't stay
with their parents at all.
Orangutans only give birth
once every seven to eight
years, as their babies take
this long to grow up.

COMPOUND SEQUENCES

Look carefully at the sequences below. Can you work out
which shapes are missing from each sequence?

A.

B.

C.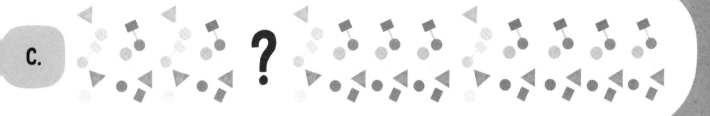

A 'compound' consists of two or
more elements bound together. For
example, sodium and chlorine are
elements. When bound together,
they make sodium chloride, which
is better known as salt.

A 'mixture' is where two or more
elements or compounds meet but
don't bond together. For example,
salt water is a mixture of salt
molecules and water molecules.

STRANDED

Can you make it through the grid to complete the game? Follow the DNA strands in the order shown in the top panel from start to finish. You can move across, up and down but not diagonally.

START

FINISH

Your DNA is completely unique and is what makes you who you are! DNA code is made up of four nitrogen bases: adenine, thymine, cytosine and guanine.

The DNA code in all humans is 99.9% the same. The remaining 0.1% is the part that is different for everyone and causes variations in people's looks and health.

FOLLOW THE FLIGHT

Can you guide this aeroplane to the finish square? Use the clues and key to find out which direction to travel in at each landmark you encounter.

1. When you reach a beach, fly south.
2. When you reach a town, fly north.
3. When you reach a pool, fly west.
4. When you reach palm trees, fly east.

KEY

N W E S

BEACH   TOWN   POOL   PALM TREES

START

FINISH

The idea of human flight has been around for centuries. The earliest known flying machine was drawn and tested by Leonardo da Vinci way back in 1490.

Air moves more quickly over the top of an aeroplane's wing than the bottom. This means there is higher air pressure below the wing than above it, allowing the plane to lift into the air and take flight.

WEATHER WARNING

Can you find the following groups of weather in the grid below?

A place's average weather conditions over a long period are called its 'climate'. Deserts often have a hot, dry climate, but can still sometimes have rainy weather.

A five-day forecast can predict the weather correctly about 90% of the time. Ten-day forecasts only get it right around half the time.

SPACE JAM

Can you help this spacecraft get to the space station and then to the Moon? They must avoid any paths that are blocked by space junk.

START

Over 500,000 pieces of human-made space junk are estimated to be circling our planet. This includes bits of rockets, tools and even an old spatula.

FINISH

The Earth's atmosphere is bombarded by dust and debris from space every day. Once every year or so, an asteroid the size of a car enters the Earth's atmosphere and burns up before it reaches the surface.

41

CONDUCTORS AND INSULATORS

Count how many of the items from the checklist you can find in this kitchen.
Does your total match the number shown?

CHECKLIST

| TABLE MAT | FRYING PAN | SLOTTED SPOON | KETTLE | WOODEN SPOON | OVEN GLOVE |

TOTAL = 24

A conductor is an object that electricity can pass through. If electricity cannot pass through it, it's an insulator.

Most metals are conductors, while most non-metals are insulators. Can you work out which of the kitchen items are conductors and which ones are insulators?

The electrical plugs in your home have metal parts to act as conductors. These allow the electricity to flow from your wall socket and into your electrical devices.

HUMAN BODY QUIZ

Put your knowledge of the human body to the test.

1. Where in the human body is the smallest bone found?
   a. Ear **b.** Mouth **c.** Hands

2. What is the heaviest organ in the human body?
   a. Liver **b.** Brain **c.** Skin

3. What type of joint is your thumb joint?
   a. Hinge **b.** Saddle **c.** Ball-and-socket

4. How many bones are there in an adult human body?
   a. 78 **b.** 152 **c.** 206

5. From which organ does oxygen enter the bloodstream?
   a. Brain **b.** Lungs **c.** Liver

6. What is the longest bone in the human body?
   a. Spine **b.** Femur **c.** Collarbone

7. Which of these muscles is the strongest?
   a. Buttocks **b.** Hamstrings **c.** Biceps

8. How many main senses does the human body have?
   a. Two **b.** Five **c.** Seven

9. Where in the body are new blood cells made?
   a. Bones **b.** Liver **c.** Brain

10. How many milk teeth does a child normally have?
    a. 48 **b.** 20 **c.** 10

CLASSIFYING CREATURES

Can you match these creatures to their classification group?
Each group must contain one creature.

Classification groups are used by scientists to sort
animals into their different families. For example, dogs
are mammals, while snakes are reptiles.

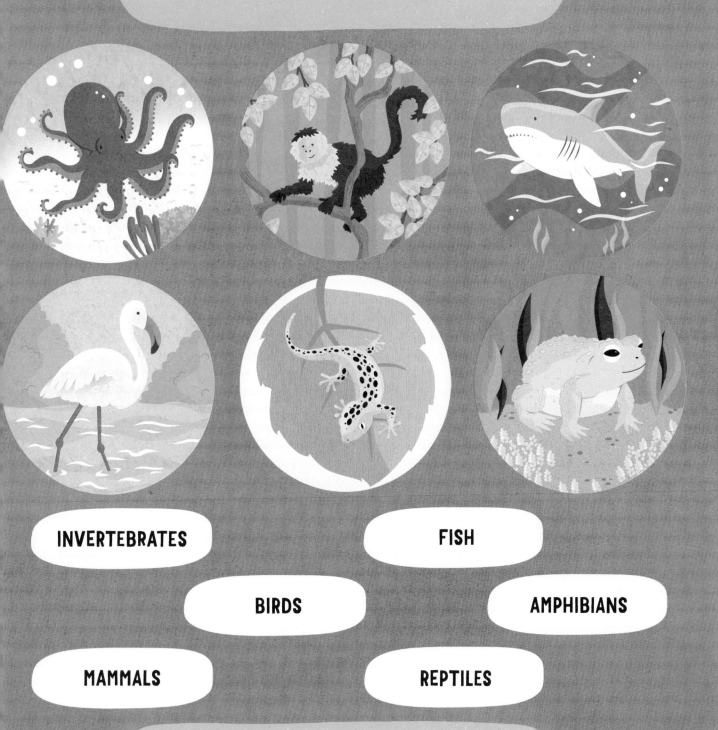

INVERTEBRATES

FISH

BIRDS

AMPHIBIANS

MAMMALS

REPTILES

Did you know that you are a mammal, as well
as a human? Mammals are animals that produce milk
for their young, and often (but not always) have hair or fur.

Find the one key that isn't part of a pair.

Around 75% of the elements on the periodic table are metals. Even calcium and iron, which are commonly found in food, are metals.

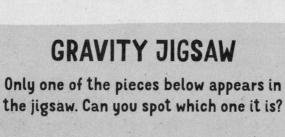

GRAVITY JIGSAW

Only one of the pieces below appears in the jigsaw. Can you spot which one it is?

A.

B.

Gravity doesn't just hold down objects. It also holds down the planet's atmosphere and oxygen. Without gravity, life on Earth would be impossible.

'Gravity' is the force by which an object, such as a planet, draws other objects towards it. It's because of gravity that if you throw a ball up in the air, it comes back down.

C.

D.

E.

FLOAT OR SINK?

'Buoyancy' is the ability something has to float in water. A beach ball is very buoyant, whereas a marble is not buoyant at all. This is because the ball is filled with air, which is less dense than the water. Take a look at the objects on board this fishing boat and work out which ones would be buoyant in the water.

Buoyancy was first described by Archimedes, an ancient Greek mathematician. The Archimedes screw, which is a machine used for raising water, is still used around the world today.

IRON NAILS

MOBILE PHONE

SPONGE

BAG OF COINS

LIFE JACKET

PIECE OF WOOD

Why do large pieces of metal sink, but metal boats float? A boat's shape is extremely important. Even though a boat is very heavy, it also has a lot of air in the middle, which allows it to float.

ENERGY SPOT THE DIFFERENCE

Can you spot ten differences between these scenes showing oil reserves at the bottom of the sea?

'Non-renewable energy' comes from sources that will run out and cannot be quickly replenished. Oil reserves, for example, take millions of years of underground heat and pressure to be created.

Most non-renewable energy resources are fossil fuels. These are formed from the fossils of plants and algae that lived hundreds of millions of years ago. Fossil fuels include coal, petroleum oil and natural gas.

ANIMAL DOT TO DOT

Join up the dots to complete this picture of a critically endangered animal. Do you know what it's called?

The International Union for Conservation of Nature (IUCN) regularly assesses species to determine which ones are vulnerable. Of the 116,000 species they have looked at, over 31,000 are threatened with extinction.

Threatened species fall into one of three classifications: vulnerable, endangered or critically endangered. A critically endangered animal is at the highest risk of becoming extinct.

Factors that can cause a species of animal to become vulnerable include over-hunting by humans, disease, destruction of habitat and climate change.

TOUCH SECTIONS

Can you divide the page into four separate sections, using just three straight lines? Each section must contain one of each sensory toy.

Unlike your senses of smell, sight, hearing and taste, your 'touch receptors' are spread across all of your skin. They send signals to your brain to help you react to different sensations of touch.

Your touch receptors are specialized, meaning that each one responds to certain types of touch. Some respond to pressure or vibration, while others respond to very delicate contact.

FOLLOW THE FUNCTION

Follow the lines to take the animal cells and plant cells to their correct function.

ANIMAL CELLS

FAT CELL   BONE-MAKING CELL   CILIATED CELL   SECRETORY CELL

This cell's long strands help it to connect to other cells.

Hormones are released by this cell.

The droplet of stored fat provides energy.

The hair-like cilia waft particles away from airways.

PLANT CELLS

STARCH-STORING CELL   LEAF CELL   SUPPORTING CELL   FRUIT CELL

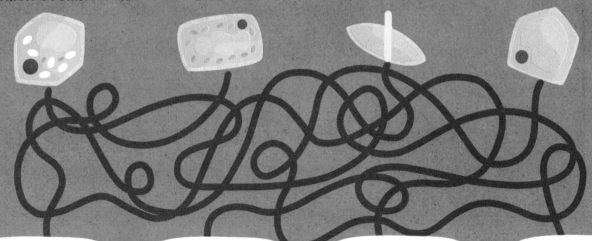

This cell helps to support a plant's stem.

This cell stores energy-rich starch.

Green chloroplasts inside this cell make food for the plant.

This cell helps to make a plant's fruit juicy.

Plant and animal cells are tiny. They range from 1 to 100 micrometres. That means anywhere from 100 to 1,000 cells can fit across the tip of a pen.

CLOWNING AROUND

These clowns got lost at the funfair and ended up in the House of Mirrors. Match each clown with its mirror-image twin.

Reflection occurs when light hits a surface and bounces off it. This happens not only with mirrors, but also with lots of other smooth surfaces, including water and even metal.

When reflection happens, light hits the smooth surface and bounces off at the same angle. This is called the law of reflection.

53

DIGESTION DUEL

Can you race a friend through the digestive system below
and out the other side? Use a button or a coin for each
player's counter and roll a dice on each go.

START

Bleugghh!
You get vomited
back up.
Start again.

Yuck! You get spat
back out. Go back
and start again.

Cough! Splutter!
You're a choking
hazard. Miss a go.

Your digestive system
moves food and water
through your body.
It also breaks nutrients
into smaller molecules,
making it easier for your
body to absorb them.

Whoosh!
A drink of water
washes you down.
Move forward
four spaces.

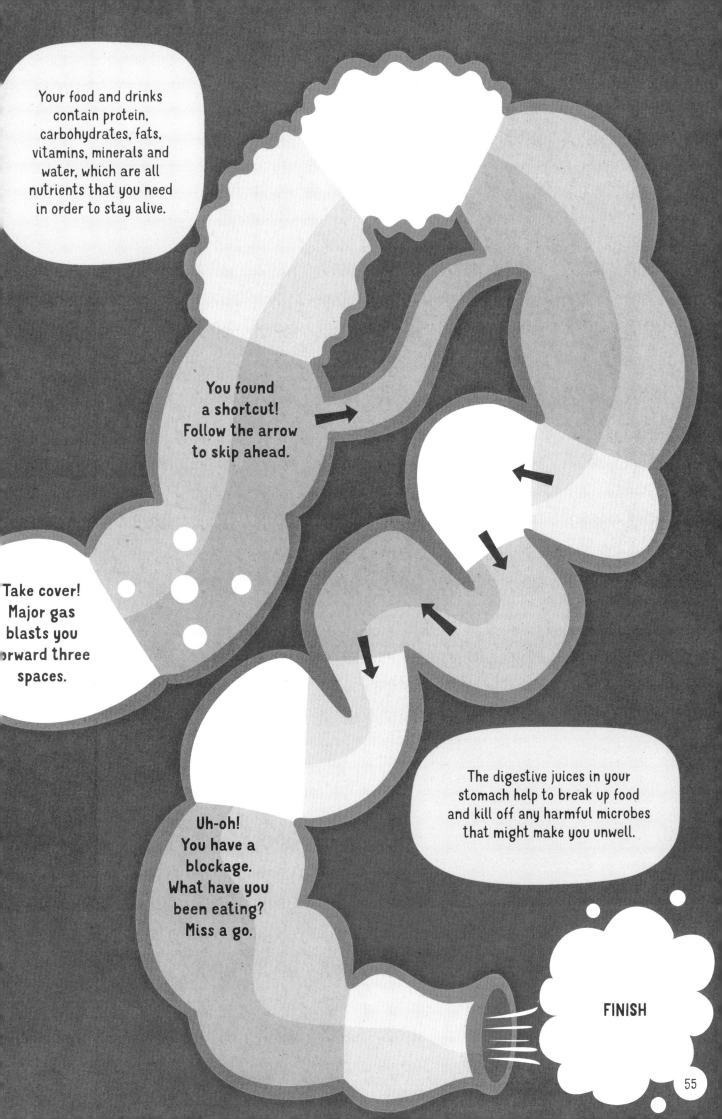

EARTH QUIZ

Put your knowledge of the planet to the test.

1. What are the two main gases in the Earth's atmosphere?
   a. Nitrogen and oxygen **b.** Oxygen and carbon dioxide
   c. Hydrogen and helium

2. What is the outer layer of the Earth's surface called?
   a. Mantle **b.** Atmosphere **c.** Crust

3. What is the largest ocean on Earth?
   a. The Pacific Ocean **b.** The Atlantic Ocean **c.** The Southern Ocean

4. What is the hot molten rock found inside the Earth called?
   a. Plasma **b.** Lava **c.** Magma

5. What is the name of a person who studies rocks?
   a. An archaeologist **b.** A biologist **c.** A geologist

6. How old is the planet Earth?
   a. 4.54 billion years old **b.** 1 billion years old **c.** 50 million years old

7. What shape is the Earth?
   a. Square **b.** Flat **c.** Bulging sphere

8. What is the scientific name for the Northern Lights?
   a. Aurora australis **b.** Aurora borealis **c.** Aurora nordis

9. What makes a rainbow?
   a. Water and heat **b.** Light and wind **c.** Water and light

10. What is the name of the highest mountain on Earth?
    a. Mount Everest **b.** K2 **c.** Nanga Parbat

FIND THE BATTERIES

Can you find all the batteries that will make these light bulbs light up? The numbers around the edge of the grid tell you how many batteries appear in each row and column. A battery can only be found horizontally or vertically next to a light bulb. Batteries are never next to each other, neither vertically, horizontally nor diagonally.

EXAMPLE:

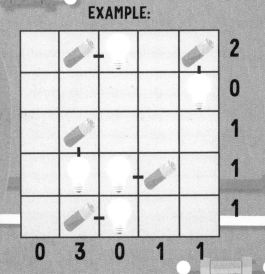

					2
					0
					1
					1
					1

0 3 0 1 1

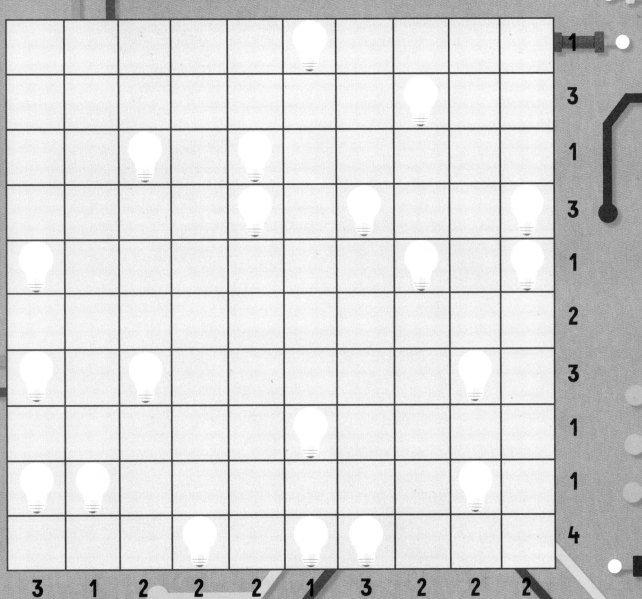

Row clues (top to bottom): 1, 3, 1, 3, 1, 2, 3, 1, 1, 4

Column clues (left to right): 3, 1, 2, 2, 2, 1, 3, 2, 2, 2

A 'battery' is a container that stores energy until it is needed. It can be used for on-the-go electronic devices, such as torches and mobile phones.

The path an electric current flows through is called an 'electrical circuit'. Every electrical circuit requires a power source, such as a battery or generator.

RUBBISH REMOVAL

Count how many of each recyclable item you spot from the checklist, then add up your answers. Does your total match the one shown?

CHECKLIST

 ALUMINIUM CAN

YOGURT POT

PLASTIC BOTTLE

CARDBOARD BOX

 NEWSPAPER

GLASS BOTTLE

TOTAL = 36

'Single-stream recycling' is where recyclable materials are gathered in a single bin, then transported to a place where they are separated out into different materials. The materials can then be used to make new products.

58

ROCKET PARTS

Circle the group below that contains all of the parts you need to make the rocket in the centre.

A.

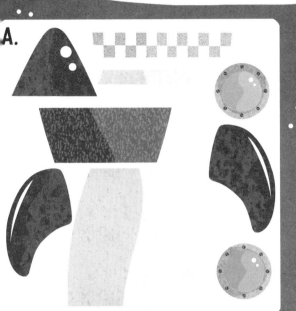

B.

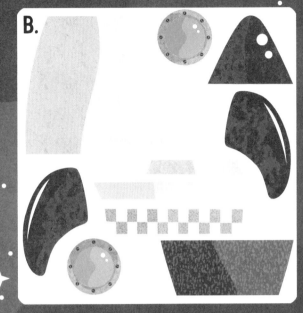

Rockets have engines, just like aeroplanes. However, because there's no oxygen in space, rockets have special parts called 'oxidizers'. These supply the oxygen rocket engines need to burn fuel.

Rockets need a lot of fuel to make it through the Earth's thick lower atmosphere. Once they are in the upper atmosphere where the air is thinner, they can drop their first engine and pointed tip to become lighter, meaning they need less fuel.

C.

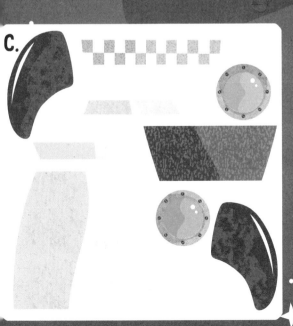

D.

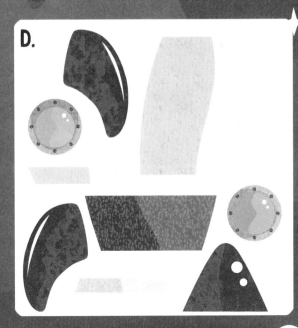

WORKBENCH JUMBLE

A scientist needs the following pieces of equipment
for an experiment. Can you find them all on the bench?

1. GOGGLES perch on the scientist's nose to help protect their eyes.
2. A MAGNIFYING GLASS is used for looking at very small objects.
3. A RING STAND has a long upright rod and holds other equipment in place.
4. A GLASS FUNNEL is used for guiding liquid into a small opening.
5. A PIPETTE is used to transfer liquid from one container to another.

Objects you can see through are 'transparent'. In transparent objects, such as glass, light is not absorbed or reflected. Instead, the object allows the light to pass right through.

Scientists often use transparent containers, such as beakers and test tubes, so that they can see any changes that take place during their experiments. A 'chemical change' is where new substances are formed. A 'physical change' is where the form of the substance changes (e.g. water changing to ice).

HOPSCOTCH SEQUENCES

Look at the number sequences on these four science-themed hopscotch games. Can you work out which numbers are missing from each sequence?

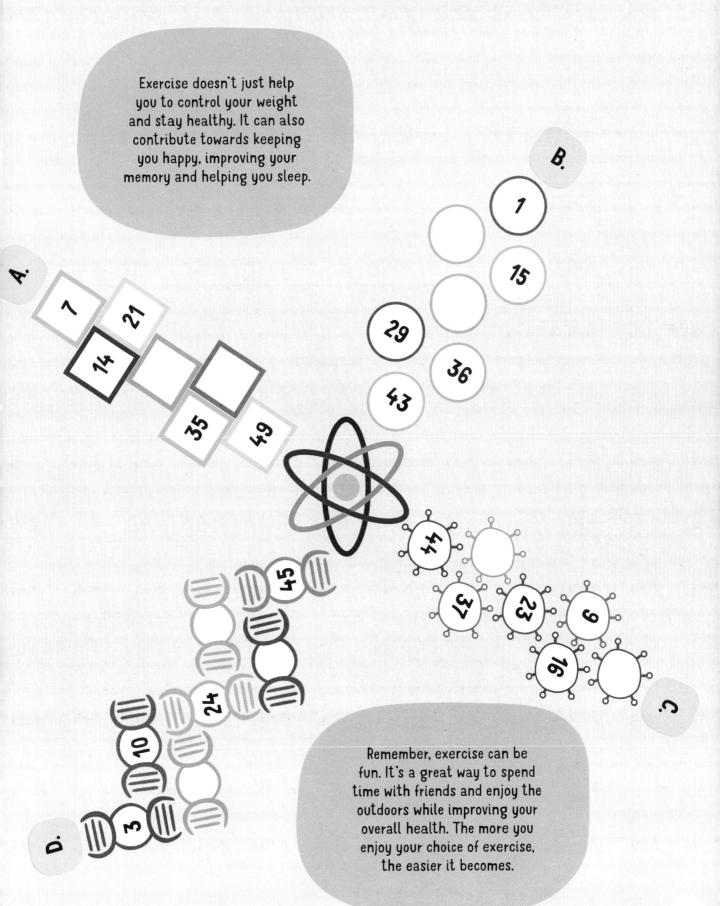

Exercise doesn't just help you to control your weight and stay healthy. It can also contribute towards keeping you happy, improving your memory and helping you sleep.

A.
7, 21, 14, __, 35, 49

B.
1, 15, 29, 36, 43

C.
44, 37, 23, 9, 16

D.
45, 24, 10, 3

Remember, exercise can be fun. It's a great way to spend time with friends and enjoy the outdoors while improving your overall health. The more you enjoy your choice of exercise, the easier it becomes.

SOUND WAVES

Noise is measured in units called decibels. Which mode of transport do you think is the noisiest? Follow the tangled lines to find out if you're right.

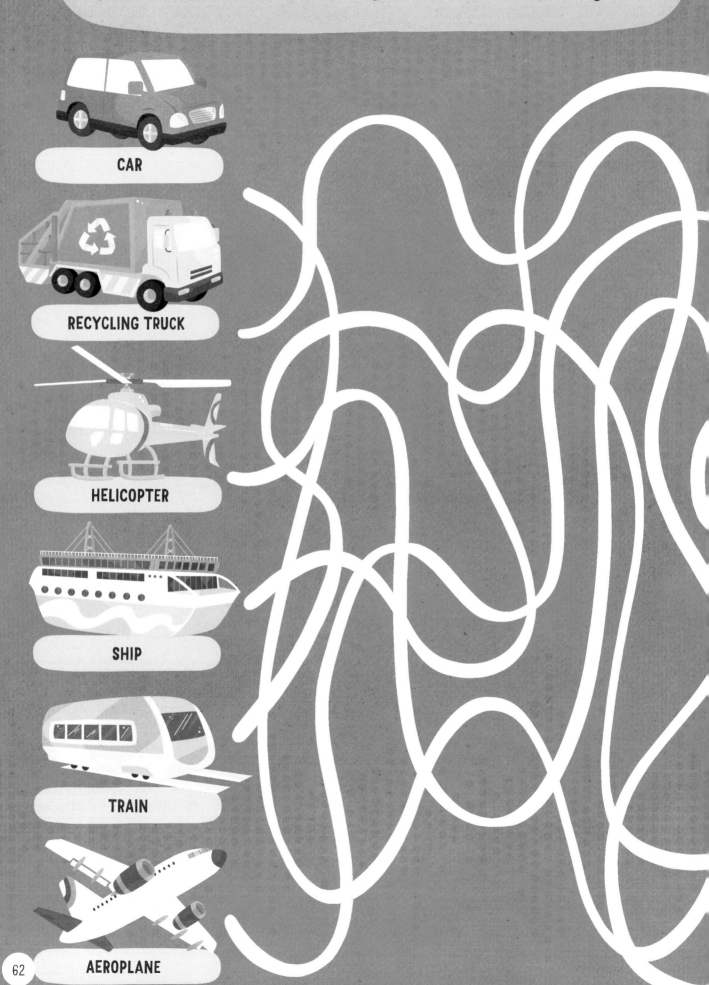

CAR

RECYCLING TRUCK

HELICOPTER

SHIP

TRAIN

AEROPLANE

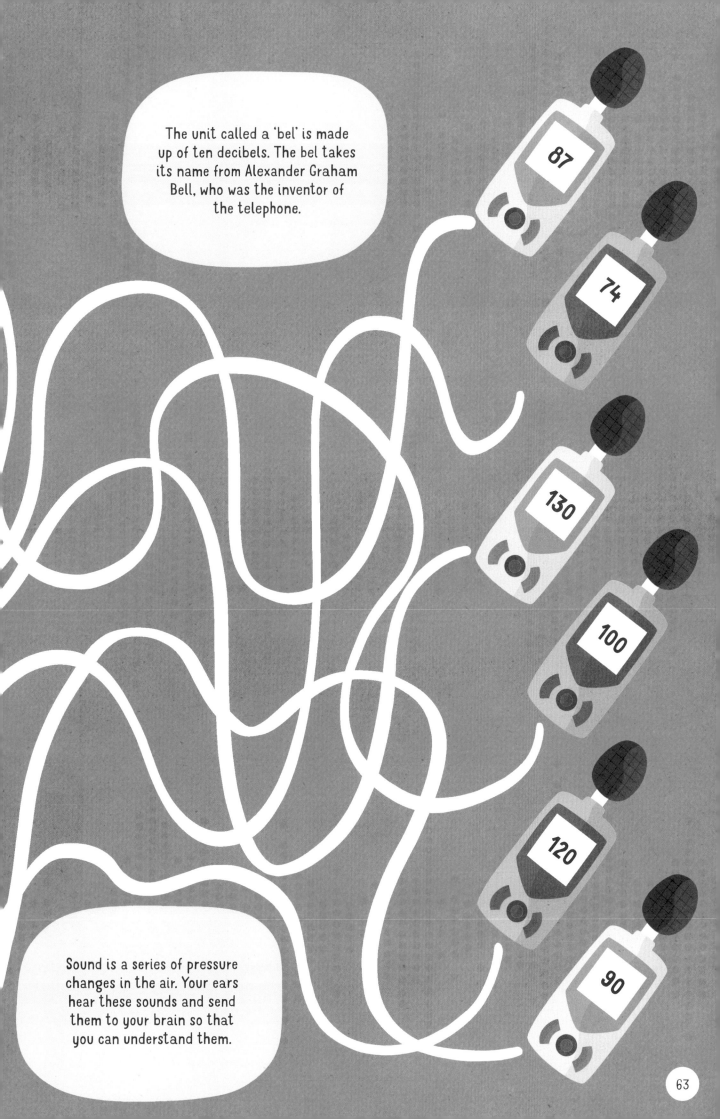

The unit called a 'bel' is made up of ten decibels. The bel takes its name from Alexander Graham Bell, who was the inventor of the telephone.

Sound is a series of pressure changes in the air. Your ears hear these sounds and send them to your brain so that you can understand them.

LET'S ROCK

Can you find the following pieces in the picture? Write their co-ordinates underneath each piece. The first one has been done for you.

H,9

Rocks are created by physical processes both underneath and on top of the Earth's surface. These include melting, cooling, deforming, compacting and eroding.

There are three kinds of rock: igneous (formed by lava and magma), sedimentary (formed by hardening of eroded rocks or pieces of living things) and metamorphic (formed by underground heat and pressure).

WHERE'S THE HARE?

Can you spot the mountain hare in this snowy scene?

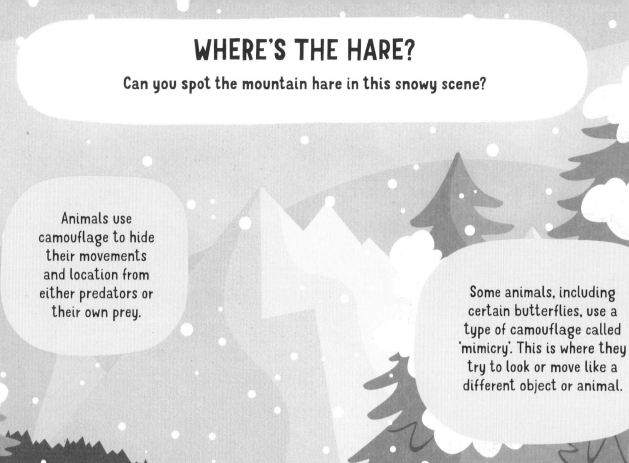

Animals use camouflage to hide their movements and location from either predators or their own prey.

Some animals, including certain butterflies, use a type of camouflage called 'mimicry'. This is where they try to look or move like a different object or animal.

Instead of using camouflage to hide, some animals use their appearance as a warning. For example, bright colours tell predators to stay away.

LIGHTNING MAZE

Can you guide this vulture between the clouds and back to its nest without touching the bolts of lightning?

START

FINISH

Storm clouds are made from a mix of hot air rising and cold air sinking. This process is called 'convection'. As the warm air cools the moisture in it condenses, creating a rain storm.

Lightning and thunder are actually produced at the exact same time. However, because light moves faster than sound, you usually see the lightning before you hear the thunder.

ODD ASTRONAUT OUT

Can you spot which astronaut has something different about their space suit?

The word 'astronaut' comes from the Greek words for 'star' and 'sailor'. People from all sorts of jobs become astronauts, including pilots, scientists and technicians.

Space suits weigh about 160 kg. They are extremely heavy on Earth, but weightless in space.

BALANCE-POD PYRAMIDS

Can you complete the number pyramids on these balance pods? Each pod contains a number that is equal to the sum of the two beneath it.

1.

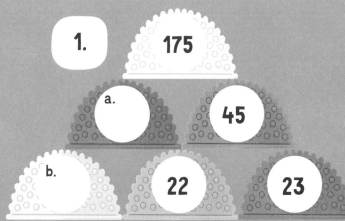

175

a.

45

b.

22

23

Two factors determine how well an object can balance: where its centre of mass is and where it touches the ground. A table with four legs is likely to balance well, but the same table with just one leg might not.

2.

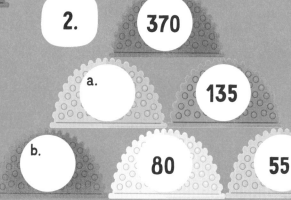

370

a.

135

b.

80

55

3.

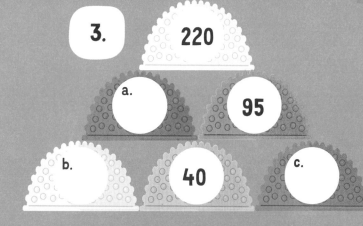

220

a.

95

b.

40

c.

Balance pods are used as exercise equipment to help improve strength, co-ordination, agility and overall balance.

4.

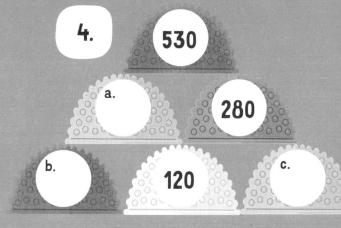

530

a.

280

b.

120

c.

ROTATING LOLLIES

Which two groups of frozen treats can be
rotated so that they match each other?

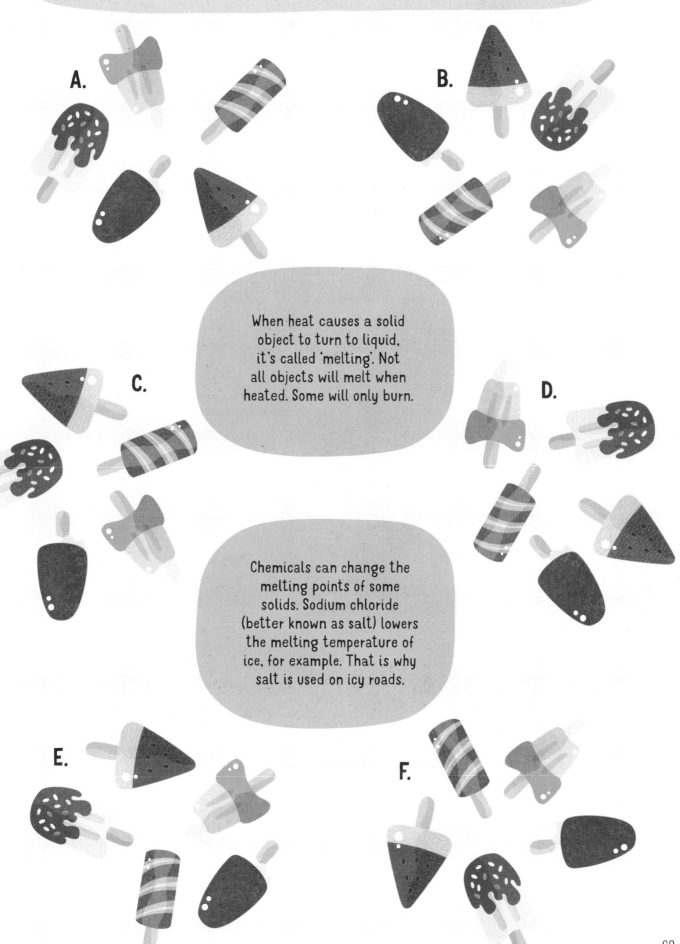

A.

B.

When heat causes a solid
object to turn to liquid,
it's called 'melting'. Not
all objects will melt when
heated. Some will only burn.

C.

D.

Chemicals can change the
melting points of some
solids. Sodium chloride
(better known as salt) lowers
the melting temperature of
ice, for example. That is why
salt is used on icy roads.

E.

F.

GENE SPOTTING

Can you spot ten differences between these family photos?

A person's 'genes' determine their hair colour, eye colour and even height.

Genetic traits can skip generations. For example, you could have brown eyes because one of your grandparents has them, even if neither of your parents do.

CYCLING CO-ORDINATES

This child is cycling home from school with his mum.
Can you answer these questions about his journey?

1. Why does he stop at B,3?
2. What does he pass at C,9?
3. What are the co-ordinates of the pond?
4. What are the co-ordinates of the play park?
5. What are the co-ordinates of the two postboxes?

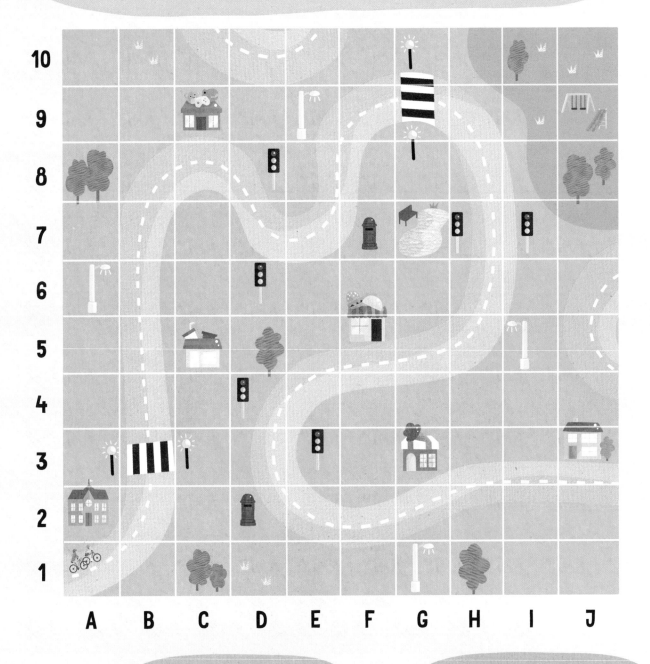

Air pollution is often invisible, but can be very harmful to human health. It is linked to higher rates of diseases such as cancer and asthma.

Cars are major producers of carbon dioxide, which is bad for the environment. That's why cycling or walking instead are great ways of reducing pollution.

PENGUIN STEPPING STONES

Guide the penguin from one side of the ice to the other.
It can only hop on to ice floes that contain multiples of 4.

Melting ice in Antarctica and Greenland is the largest cause of rising sea levels around the world. This can lead to an increase in storms and erosion worldwide, as well as loss of habitat for many animals.

FINISH

31

14

28

36

20

32

2

12

11

22

8

48

30

9

16

31

4

34

18

38

1

10

The Arctic is warming twice as fast as anywhere else on Earth. Scientists think that the Arctic could be free of ice in the summer of 2040 if climate change continues at its current rate.

6

START

FINGERPRINT FINDING

The police have found a fingerprint at the scene of a burglary. Take a look at the fingerprint and see if you can find a match from the suspects below.

'Forensic science' is the use of science to investigate crimes and present evidence to uphold the law.

The science and analysis of identifying fingerprints is called 'dactyloscopy'. Everyone has different fingerprint patterns - even identical twins.

A.

B.

C.

D.

E.

GLOW-STICK HUNT

Count how many of each kind of glow stick you can find at this birthday party. Does your total match the number shown?

CHECKLIST

TOTAL = 45

Objects don't actually have any colour – not even glow sticks! The colours you see are objects reflecting different wavelengths of light, which are seen as colour by the eye.

Scientists estimate that humans can see up to 10 million colours. However, there are colours that some animals can see that humans cannot.

CONSTELLATION CHALLENGE

Look at these constellations for one minute each and try to remember them. Then, turn the page and see if you can join the right stars to recreate the patterns.

'Constellations' are groups of stars that form distinct shapes. Constellations were identified over 6,000 years ago by people who liked to make up stories about the shapes they saw in the night sky.

CONSTELLATION CHALLENGE

Can you join the right stars to match the
patterns of the constellations on the previous page?

UNDERWATER JIGSAW

Work out which jigsaw pieces you need to complete this underwater scene.

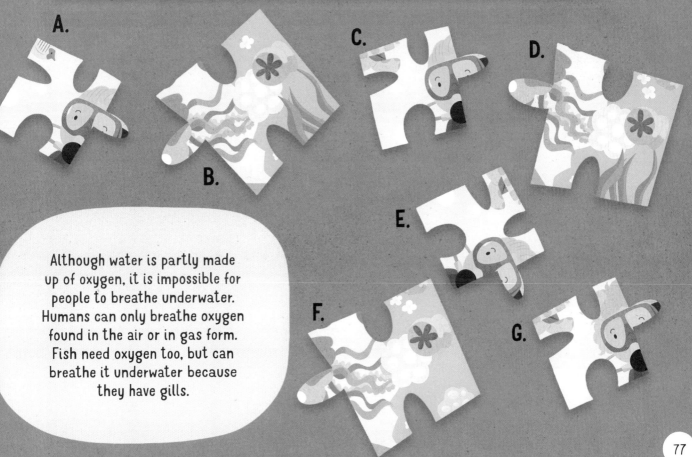

A.

B.

C.

D.

E.

F.

G.

Although water is partly made up of oxygen, it is impossible for people to breathe underwater. Humans can only breathe oxygen found in the air or in gas form. Fish need oxygen too, but can breathe it underwater because they have gills.

SOLAR-PANEL PUZZLE

Use the following clues to work out which house is having solar panels installed. The house that is having solar panels installed has ...

1. A chimney
2. No window on the roof
3. A garage door that is neither yellow nor blue

The Sun gives more energy to the Earth in one hour than everyone on the planet uses in a whole year. Solar panels can be used to provide electricity and heat homes and water.

'Renewable energy' comes from a natural unlimited resource or process, such as solar power from the Sun or wind power from the wind. Since renewable energy doesn't use polluting fossil fuels, it is sometimes called 'clean energy'.

FOOD CHAINS

'Food chains' show how nutrients are passed from one living thing to another.
Use the pictures at the bottom of the page to complete these food chains.
The first one shows you how it works.

Food chains often start with a plant or algae, and end with a predator.

SEAWEED

GRASS

RABBIT

COYOTE

CHICKEN

FISH

HAWK

LEAF

Since animals tend to eat more than one type of food, their food chains often overlap with one another. Overlapping chains are called a 'food web'.

SHARK

EARTHWORM

SEAL

79

RADIOACTIVE COUNTING

Count how many of each radioactive object you can spot from the checklist, then add up your answers. Does your total match the one shown?

CHECKLIST

TOTAL = 12

Radioactive substances give off radiation, which is very dangerous to human health. That is why it is very important for radioactive waste to be stored safely away from human contact.

MARKET MUDDLE

Follow each person around the farmers' market and find out what they buy. Be sure to avoid dead ends.

No one type of fruit or vegetable has all of the nutrients and minerals you need to stay healthy. That is why it is important to have a varied and balanced diet.

LINDA

DEV

CLARA

DALE

Fresh food is typically much better for you than frozen or canned, because it usually contains a higher variety and amount of nutrients.

SOLID, LIQUID OR GAS?

Can you sort these objects into the three categories below?

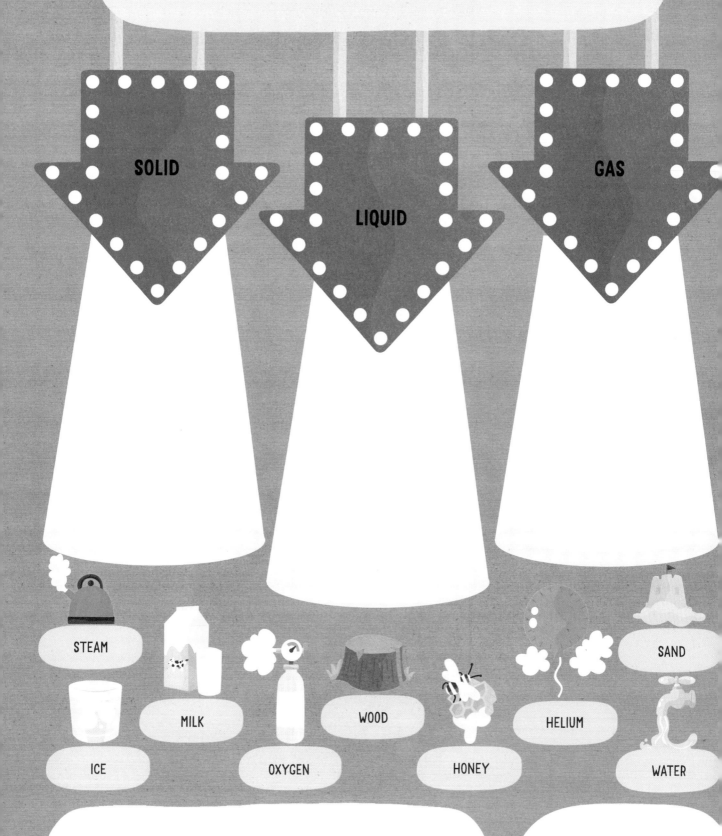

SOLID

LIQUID

GAS

STEAM

MILK

WOOD

SAND

HELIUM

ICE

OXYGEN

HONEY

WATER

Solids, liquids and gases are all made up of microscopic particles. Gas molecules move freely and at high speeds, while molecules in a solid are too tightly packed to move past each other. Liquid molecules are somewhere in between, flowing past one another at slower speeds than gas molecules.

There is actually a fourth state of matter, called 'plasma'. Plasma does not occur naturally on Earth, but can be created in a lab.

MATCHING MAGNETS

Match each magnet to its pair.

A magnet is any material that attracts iron and has its own magnetic field.

Magnets are used for a lot more than just hanging pictures on your fridge! They are also used in the making of televisions, computers and compasses.

PERIODIC PUZZLE

This section of the periodic table shows some of the common uses and sources of its elements. Can you answer the questions below? The table has been given numbers and letters so that you can work out each element's co-ordinates.

1. Which alkali metal is found at A,3?
2. What is an example of an object often made from cobalt? It's found at I,4.
3. Which halogen, found in eggs, is found at P,5?
4. Which transition metal, used in thermometers, is found at L,2?
5. Which noble gas, found at R,5, is often used in light bulbs?

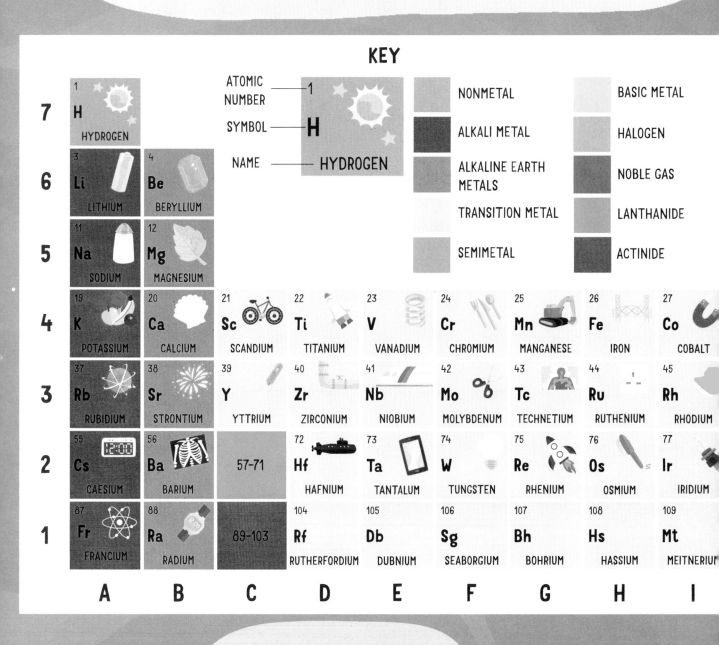

KEY

ATOMIC NUMBER

SYMBOL

NAME

	NONMETAL		BASIC METAL
	ALKALI METAL		HALOGEN
	ALKALINE EARTH METALS		NOBLE GAS
	TRANSITION METAL		LANTHANIDE
	SEMIMETAL		ACTINIDE

A **B** **C** **D** **E** **F** **G** **H** **I**

A Russian chemist called Dmitri Mendeleev developed the first version of the periodic table in 1869. Since then, many elements have been discovered and added to the table.

Chlorine, found in the table at Q,5, is often used to purify water. It is used in both swimming pools and water treatment plants.

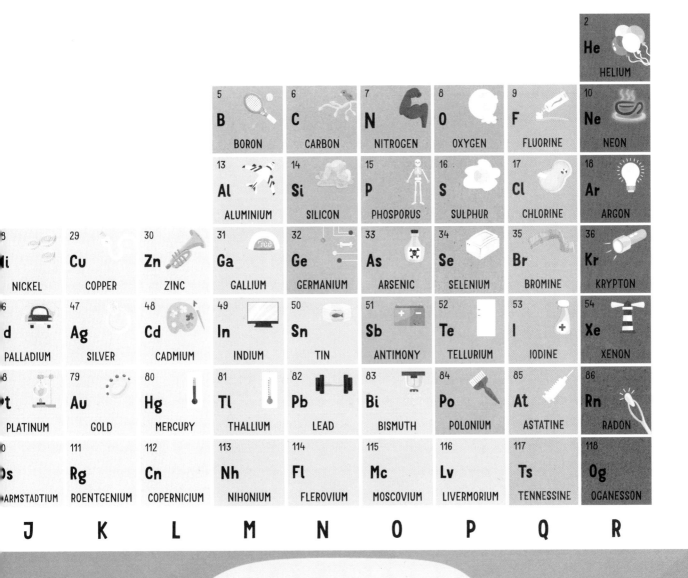

			2 He HELIUM
5 B BORON	6 C CARBON	7 N NITROGEN	8 O OXYGEN	9 F FLUORINE	10 Ne NEON

J K L M N O P Q R

Elements are positioned on the table in order of their atomic number. For example, hydrogen (A,7) has the atomic number one. This is because hydrogen has one proton.

PLANTS QUIZ

Put your knowledge of all things green and leafy to the test.

1. Which of these plants spread their seeds on water?
   a. Dandelions **b.** Water lilies **c.** Roses

2. What are leaves for?
   a. To protect plants from the rain **b.** To make plants look pretty
   c. To soak up the Sun's energy and convert it into food

3. How does a plant get water from the soil?
   a. Through its leaves **b.** Through its flowers **c.** Through its roots

4. How can you tell the age of a tree?
   a. By counting the rings inside its trunk **b.** By measuring its height
   c. By counting its leaves

5. Where would you normally find algae?
   a. In water **b.** On wood **c.** In buildings

6. What is the male part of a flower called?
   a. Pollen **b.** Stamen **c.** Carpel

7. How does pollen move from flower to flower?
   a. Wind and bees **b.** Water and bees **c.** Wind, water and bees

8. What colour is most commonly associated with lavender?
   a. Brown **b.** Purple **c.** Red

9. Only one of these is a plant – which one?
   a. Sea cucumber **b.** Coral **c.** Monkey puzzle

10. What is a deciduous plant?
    a. A plant that bears fruit
    b. A plant that loses its leaves each year
    c. A plant that stays green all year

BAFFLING BRIDGES

Can you guide this scientist home from her laboratory?
Avoid the broken bridges and road closures along the way.

START

FINISH

Bridges are able to hold a great amount of weight due to two forces: 'compression' and 'tension'. Compression is when two materials are squeezed together, while tension pulls materials apart.

The longest bridge in the world is the Danyang-Kunshan Grand Bridge in China. It's 164 km long. That's the length of 1,560 football pitches.

ODD SOCKS

Can you find the two socks that have no matching pair?

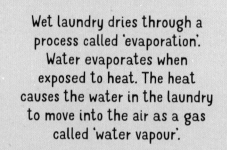

Wet laundry dries through a process called 'evaporation'. Water evaporates when exposed to heat. The heat causes the water in the laundry to move into the air as a gas called 'water vapour'.

The opposite of evaporation is 'condensation'. This is when water vapour from the air forms a liquid. An example is the wet dew you sometimes find on grass in the morning, even when it hasn't been raining.

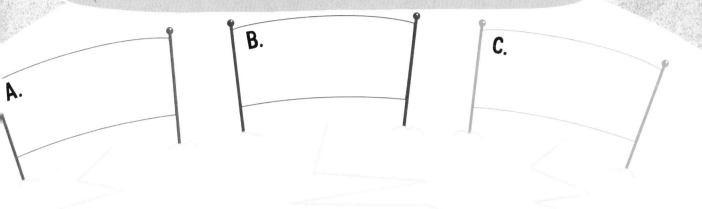

SKI SEASON

Follow the lines to see where each person started from, and write their names on the banners.

A.

B.

C.

SAM

RHONA

ANYA

A skier's downhill speed is impacted by 'kinetic friction'. The amount of kinetic friction depends on many factors. For example, there is usually more friction on a rough surface than a smooth one.

The larger the mass of the skier, the faster they travel. However, as their speed increases, so too will the level of kinetic friction, which will eventually slow them down.

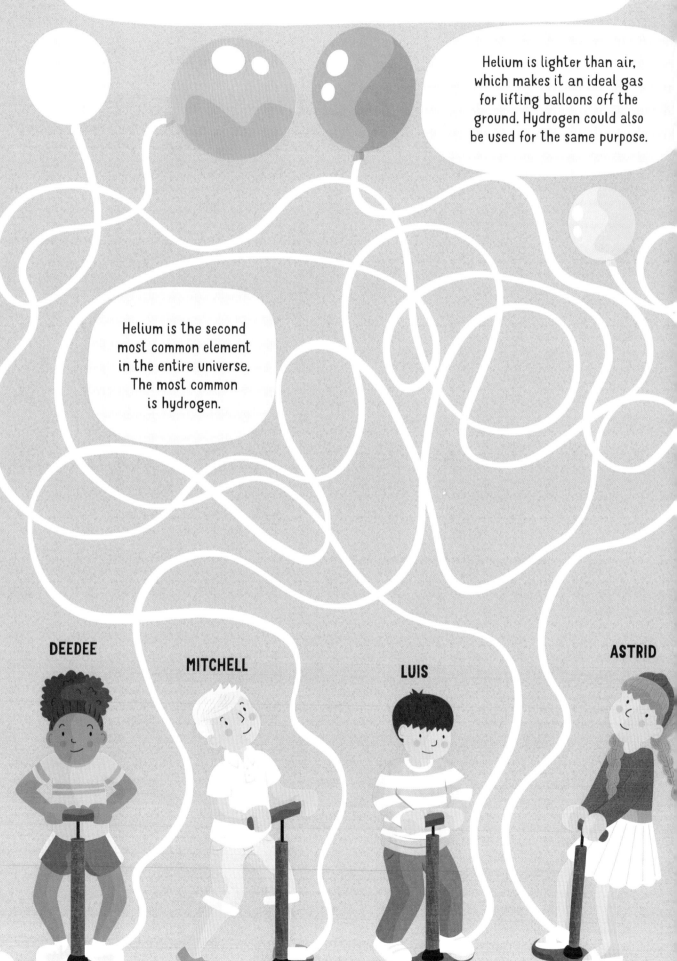

DRONE CLOSE-UPS

These drones have taken photographs of different trees.
Can you work out which drone took which photograph?

A.

B.

C.

D.

Drones are extremely useful to scientists. They have been used to predict flooding, detect disease among forest trees and monitor the spread of algae in water.

Drones are controlled by either a person on the ground or an onboard computer. Drones are used for many purposes, including photography and tree-replanting projects.

DIGGING FOR DINOSAURS

These paleontologists are digging for dinosaur fossils.
Can you spot ten differences between the two scenes?

A 'fossil' is a trace or impression of an animal or plant that has become preserved in rock. Some fossils are millions of years old.

Scientists can use fossils to find out information about what the world was like long before humans were around. People have been studying dinosaur fossils since the 1800s.

NEED FOR SPEED

Circle the group below that contains all of the parts that you need to make this racing car.

'Speed' and 'velocity' can both be used to measure the movement of a vehicle. Speed is the time rate at which the vehicle is travelling (e.g. kilometres per hour), while velocity is a combination of speed and direction.

Since velocity is both the speed and direction of an object, either the speed or direction must change for the velocity to change. To change the speed or direction, a force, such as a push or pull, is needed.

A.

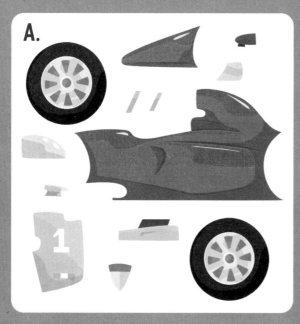

B.

C.

D.

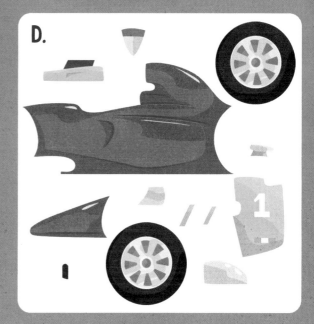

CLIMBING HIGH

**Join the dots to reveal the world's highest mountain.
Do you know what the mountain is called?**

As you climb higher up a mountain, the air gets thinner and the climate changes. Mountains typically get about one degree Celsius cooler for every 165 metres in height.

Mountain animals have different ways of coping with harsh winters. Marmots, for example, will hibernate, while mountain goats move to lower levels to find easier conditions.

Towards the tops of high mountains, plants become smaller because of the thinner air. On very high mountains you will even reach a point where plants don't grow at all and you only find snow.

VERTEBRATE VERSUS INVERTEBRATE

Help the frog and snail get to the central lily pad by drawing a line between the stepping stones. The frog can only hop on stepping stones with answers that are even numbers and the snail can only climb on to stones with answers that are odd numbers.

Frogs are 'vertebrates', while snails are 'invertebrates'. All animals are either one or the other. Vertebrates have backbones, while invertebrates do not have backbones.

Many invertebrates have something called an 'exoskeleton'. An exoskeleton is a hard skeleton on the outside of the body that protects the creature's soft insides.

8   2   24   9   12   13   4   25   10   6   7   29   14   3

UNDER THREAT

Only two of these threatened animals are on the right track for the river. Follow the paths to find out which ones.

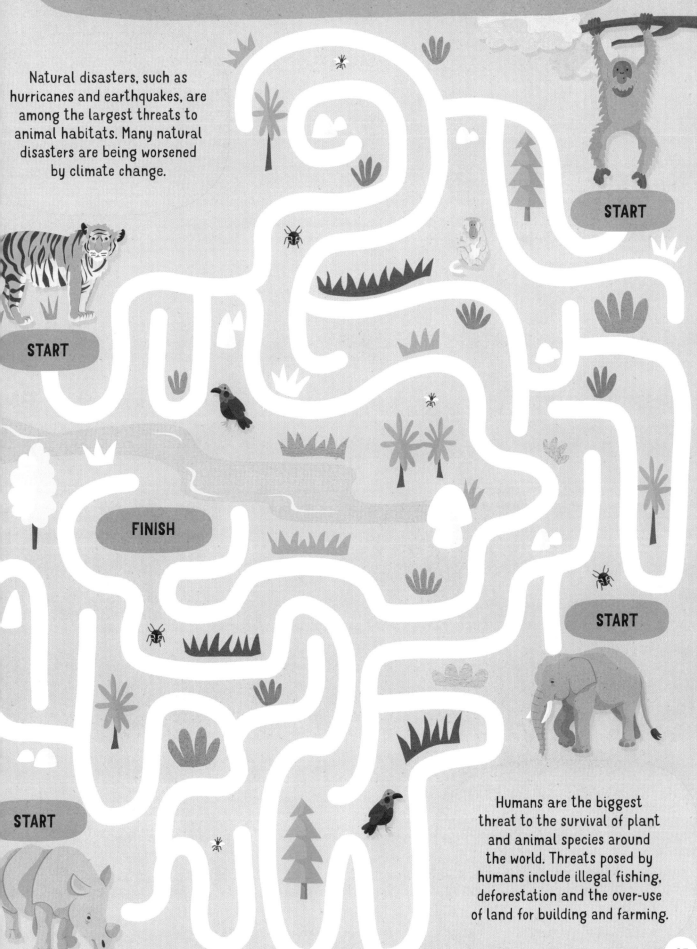

Natural disasters, such as hurricanes and earthquakes, are among the largest threats to animal habitats. Many natural disasters are being worsened by climate change.

START

START

START

FINISH

START

START

Humans are the biggest threat to the survival of plant and animal species around the world. Threats posed by humans include illegal fishing, deforestation and the over-use of land for building and farming.

MICRO-DOKU

Fill in the two sudoku grids with these six microorganisms. Each row, column and six-square block must only contain one of each type.

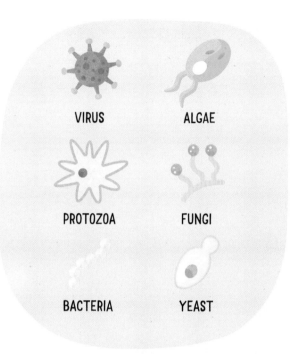

VIRUS   ALGAE

PROTOZOA   FUNGI

BACTERIA   YEAST

EXAMPLE:

1.

2.

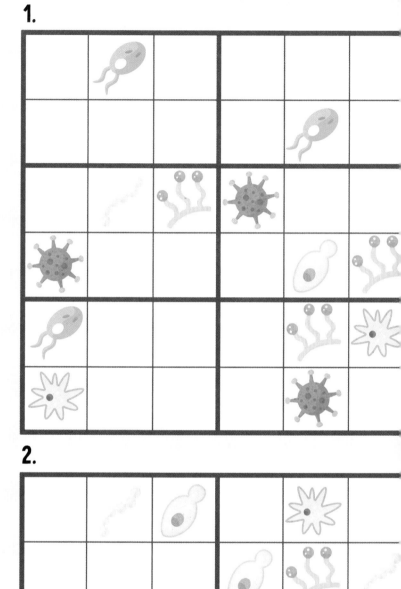

'Microorganisms', or 'microbes', are very simple forms of life. They are so small that they can only be seen with a microscope.

WAY OF THE WATER

Can you find the following pieces in the water cycle diagram? Write the co-ordinates underneath each piece. The first one has been done for you.

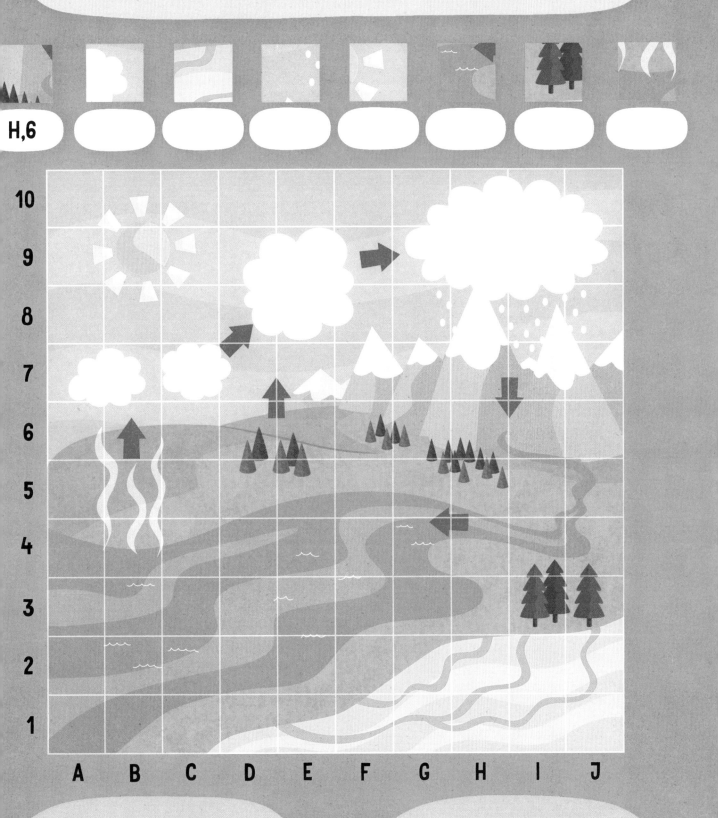

H,6

The water cycle shows how water moves around an ecosystem by evaporating into the air and eventually falling again as 'precipitation' (rain or snow, for example).

Water (or lack of water) influences climate cycles and is often a key part of extreme events, such as drought and flooding.

DISCOVERY MIX-UP

Below are some incredible scientific discoveries,
but they are all placed underneath the wrong picture.
Can you work out which fact belongs with which image?

Carl Wilhelm Scheele discovered oxygen in 1773. He used an instrument that heated a chemical mixture and collected the oxygen in a bag tied to the end.

Andre Geim and Kostya Novoselov discovered graphene in 2004. It is only one atom thick, making it the thinnest known material.

Our prehistoric ancestors discovered fire around 1.5 million years ago. It became vital for heat, light and protection from predators.

Marie and Pierre Curie discovered the elements radium and polonium in 1898. Marie became the first woman to win a Nobel Prize.

In 1878, Hilaire de Chardonnet discovered that the fabric rayon can be used to make synthetic silk.

John Dalton was the first person to provide evidence for the existence of the atom, in 1803.

TINY TREES

Read the clues to discover which of the five trees is the youngest.

1. The youngest tree has green leaves.
2. It is not the smallest tree.
3. It does not have the narrowest trunk.

For trees to grow, seeds must first be planted or spread, either by an animal, the wind or water. If the seed settles in a good spot, it will start as a young sprout, growing its roots downward to anchor into the soil.

As a tree sprout continues to grow, it starts to take on a more woody appearance and becomes a seedling. Trees are seedlings for a few years before growing into saplings and eventually mature trees.

A. B. C. D. E.

WEIGHING PARCELS

These scales measure weight in grams (g) and kilograms (kg). There are 1,000 grams in a kilogram. Check the scales for each of these parcels and write their weights in the spaces provided.

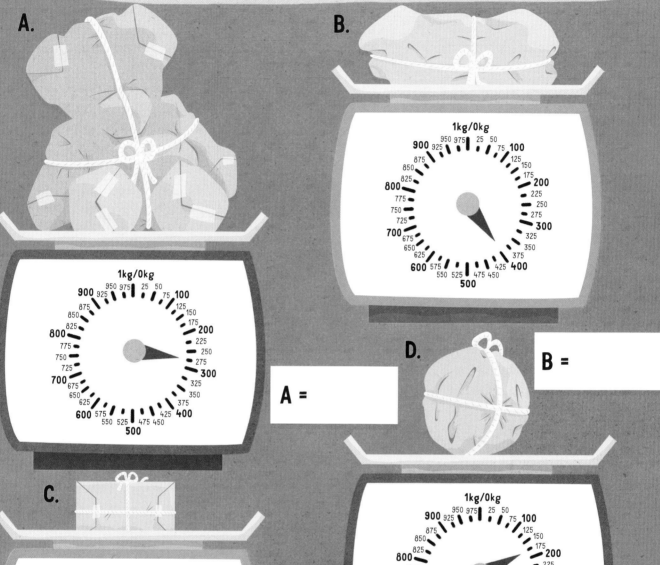

A.

B.

A =

B =

D.

C.

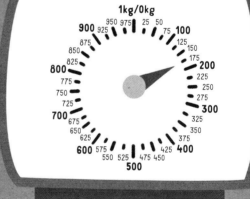

C =

D =

Did you know your weight is six times greater on Earth than it would be if you were on the Moon? That's because the Earth has a much stronger gravitational pull than the Moon.

When astronauts are in space there is no gravitational pull, so they have no weight. That is why astronauts are seen floating while on space walks.

ERUPTING VOLCANOS

Can you match each erupting volcano to its silhouette?

Volcanoes typically lie along the edges of 'tectonic plates', which are large, moving pieces of the Earth's crust.

A volcano is an opening in the Earth's crust where molten rock, known as 'magma', rises to the surface. Magma that has reached the surface is called lava.

ROLLER-COASTER RIDE

Guide the cart along the tracks to the end of the ride.
You cannot pass the other carts.

Roller-coasters use both 'potential' and 'kinetic' energy. Potential energy is stored energy that can produce motion, while kinetic energy is used when the object is moving.

When a roller-coaster is at the top of the slope, it has potential energy. As it moves down, the potential energy is converted to kinetic energy. The roller-coaster reaches its fastest speed at the bottom of the slope when it is using only kinetic energy.

FINISH

BALANCED DIET

It's time to cook a healthy, balanced meal. Read the recipe cards below and work out which one uses all the ingredients shown at the bottom of the page.

A.
1 can of chopped tomatoes
1 butternut squash
2 red peppers
1 bunch of coriander
Dried apricots
2 red onions
1 can of chickpeas
Pomegranate seeds

It is important to maintain a balanced diet. This means including all of the main food groups in your daily meals. Around half of your plate should consist of fruits and vegetables. The more colour, the better!

B.
1 butternut squash
1 bunch of coriander
Dried apricots
2 red peppers
2 red onions
Quinoa
1 can of chopped tomatoes
Pomegranate seeds

C.
2 red peppers
2 red onions
1 butternut squash
1 bunch of coriander
1 can of chickpeas
1 can of chopped tomatoes
Quinoa
Dried apricots
Pomegranate seeds

A balanced diet is not only nutritious, but can also help to protect you from conditions such as heart disease, diabetes and cancer. The younger you adopt healthy eating practices, the better off you will be.

RED ONIONS

BUTTERNUT SQUASH

CHICKPEAS

CORIANDER

QUINOA

CHOPPED TOMATOES

POMEGRANATE SEEDS

RED PEPPERS

DRIED APRICOTS

MATCHING MINERALS

Match each mineral to its shadow.

Minerals are the crystals that make up rocks. Each different mineral has a very specific chemical make-up. This allows scientists to tell one mineral from another.

There are over 4,000 naturally occurring minerals on Earth. They differ not only in chemical make-up, but also in colour, hardness and even magnetism.

The most common mineral in the Earth's crust is called 'feldspar'. Feldspar is formed from volcanic activity and is commonly used to make glass and ceramics.

CONGO COUNTING

Count how many of the following animals you find in the Congo Basin rainforest. When you add them all up, your total should match the number shown.

CHECKLIST

GORILLA

LEOPARD

CONGO SERPENT EAGLE

TREE PANGOLIN

WILD AFRICAN GREY PARROT

OKAPI

TOTAL = 27

'Deforestation' is when humans clear forests to use the land for other purposes. Around the world, a forest area the size of 30 football pitches is cleared every minute.

Forests are home to 80% of the world's land species, including plants, animals, fungi and bacteria.

Forests provide much of the oxygen that all living things on Earth need to survive.

ALLOYS BRAIN-TEASER

Can you find the following groups of instruments in the grid below?

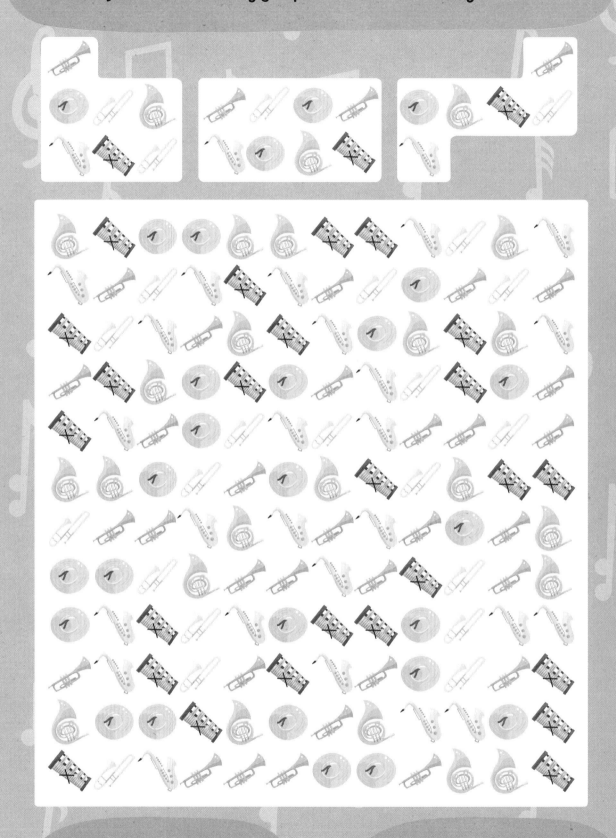

An 'alloy' is a metal made by combining two or more metallic elements. Alloys aren't found in nature, but created by melting the elemental ingredients together.

Brass, an alloy made of copper and zinc, is commonly used to make musical instruments. Brass instruments include the trumpet, trombone, French horn and tuba.

ANIMALS: TRUE OR FALSE?

Put your knowledge of animals to the test. Which of the following facts are true and which are false?

1. A group of fish is called a shoal.

2. All mammals live on land.

3. Elephants are born after nine months in the mother's womb.

4. Great white sharks have such a strong sense of smell that they can detect a colony of seals two miles away.

5. Horses and zebras are odd-toed hoofed mammals.

6. Many fish give birth by laying eggs.

7. Baby mammals drink their mother's milk.

8. Anteaters vacuum up ants with their noses.

9. A beaver has a set of lips behind its front teeth.

10. Fish breathe by pulling oxygen into their lungs.

CHEMICAL REACTIONS

Can you spot ten differences between these two laboratory experiments?

A chemical reaction is when two or more substances interact to form a new substance. For example, when you mix metal caesium with water you create an explosion of hydrogen gas and caesium hydroxide. This can break the container!

Chemical reactions can be both natural and human-made. The burning of fuels, formation of minerals and even manufacturing of cheese all involve chemical reactions.

In chemical reactions, the substances going through the reaction are called 'reactants', and the end results are called 'products'.

BONE UP

Only one of the groups below contains all of the bones needed to make this skeleton foot. Can you work out which one it is?

Human babies are born with about 300 bones in their bodies, but these bones join together to become 206 bones by adulthood.

A skeleton doesn't just give a body its structure. It also protects soft internal organs. For example, the rib cage protects the heart and lungs, and the skull protects the brain.

A.

B.

C.

D.

DOTTY BODY PART

Join up the dots to complete this picture of a part of the human body. Do you know what it's called?

The 'nervous system' is a collection of nerves and nerve cells that send signals through the body.

Your senses take signals from your nervous system so that you know to react. For example, if you touch a hot plate, you'll know to pull your hand back.

Human nerves are all connected to the brain and spinal cord.

TUG OF WAR

These children are playing a game of tug of war. Each team member has a number on their shirt. The team with the highest total number will win the game. Can you work out which team is going to win?

In a tug of war, if two teams with the same amount of strength pull on each end of the rope, the force is balanced.

When one team has extra force at one end of the rope, the force is unbalanced. The unbalanced force is what allows one side to win.

ALL THE ANSWERS

COUNTING IN THE LAB P4–5

There are: **5** conical flasks, **6** bunsen burners, **10** test tubes, **3** safety goggles, **12** gloves and **7** petri dishes.

TURNING TURBINE P6

ACID OR ALKALI? P7

Lemons: **2**   Soap: **12**
Soda: **3**   Broccoli: **10**
Eggs: **9**   Bleach: **13**
Bananas: **5**

SALAMANDER SHADOW P8

Shadow **D** matches the salamander's shape.

TASTE-BUD TRAIL P9

MAGNETIC MAYHEM P10

The magnetic items are: **scissors, key, padlock, spoo**
(and of course the **magnet** itself)

URINE UNCERTAINTY P11

Blocked nose: **FALSE**   Gunpowder: **TRUE**
Healthy heart: **FALSE**   Dog wee: **TRUE**
Plants: **TRUE**   Romans: **TRUE**

CRYSTAL CAVE JIGSAW P12–13

Tiles **B**, **D** and **E** appear in the scene.

MOMENTUM SEQUENCES P14

4, 8, 12, 16, **20**
10, 16, 22, 28, **34**
4, 5, 7, 10, 14

LOWER POWER P15

ESISTANCE REVEAL P16

e dots reveal a **parachute**.

ABORATORY SUDOKU P17

1.

2.

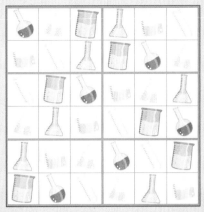

WIND TURBINE SPOT THE DIFFERENCE P18

SPACE QUIZ P19

1. a **2.** b **3.** a **4.** c **5.** b **6.** c **7.** c **8.** a **9.** c **10.** b

CROSSED WIRES P20–21

1 – D, 2 – C, 3 – F, 4 – A, 5 – B, 6 – E

SEASON SECTIONS P22

MICROSCOPE PARTS P23

Group **B** has all the correct parts.

AMAZING LIFE CYCLES P24–25

OAK TREE: acorn, **seedling**, sapling, mature oak tree
ROBIN: **egg**, hatchling, **nestling**, fledgling, juvenile,
    adult robin
BUTTERFLY: egg, **caterpillar**, **chrysalis**, adult butterfly
FROG: eggs, tadpole, tadpole with 2 legs, tadpole
    with 4 legs, **adult frog**

FORCES IN ACTION P26

A. 49 seconds
B. 11 seconds
C. 3 seconds

COMBUSTION COUNTING P27

There are: **3** rings, **4** chrysanthemums,
2 crackles, **3** whirlwinds, **5** waves and
3 glitters.

THE HEAT IS ON P28

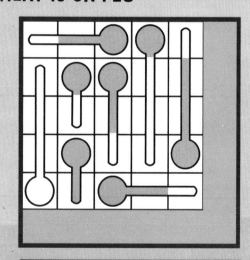

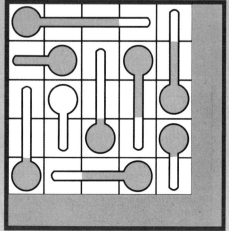

MATERIAL MATCH UP P29

WOOD: pencil   PLASTIC: ruler
GLASS: mirror   METAL: compass
RUBBER: eraser   PAPER: sticky notes

PUMP THE BLOOD P30

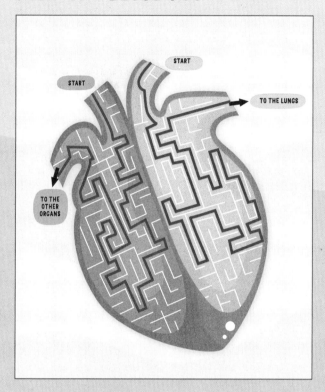

ATOMS ADDITION P31

A. 33   **C.** 37
B. 79   **D.** 68

B has the highest number of electrons.

DATA DILEMMA P32

Bar graph **B** shows the correct results.

WHAT A PONG! P33

A – 6 (Brussels sprouts)
B – 2 (egg)
C – 3 (durian fruit)
D – 4 (can of tuna)
E – 5 (raw onion)
F – 1 (cheese)

UT OF THIS WORLD P34–35

Earth   **D. Mars**   **G. Uranus**

Mercury   **E. Jupiter**   **H. Neptune**

Venus   **F. Saturn**   **I. Pluto**

ORSE AND FOAL JIGSAW P36

e D does not appear in the picture.

OMPOUND SEQUENCES P37

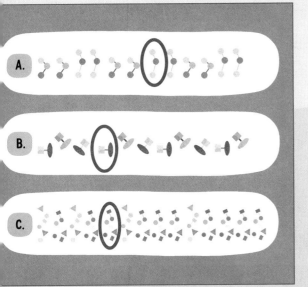

TRANDED P38

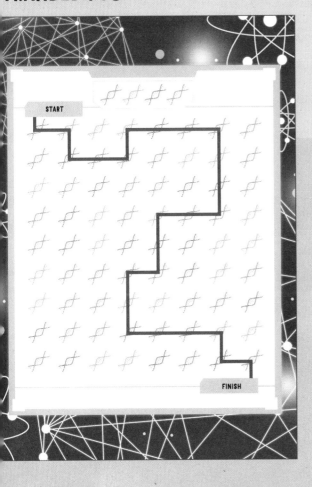

FOLLOW THE FLIGHT P39

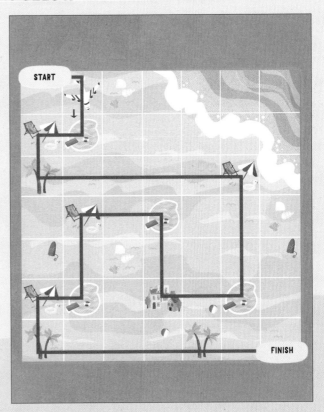

WEATHER WARNING P40

SPACE JAM P41

METAL MATCH UP P46

CONDUCTORS AND INSULATORS P42–43

There are: **5** table mats (insulator), **3** frying pans, (conductor), **5** slotted spoons (conductor), **2** kettles (conductor), **4** wooden spoons (insulator) and **5** oven gloves (insulator).

GRAVITY JIGSAW P47

Piece **C** appears in the jigsaw.

FLOAT OR SINK? P48

The **life jacket** and the **piece of wood** are buoyant. The **sponge** is also buoyant, but will sink once it takes on water.

ENERGY SPOT THE DIFFERENCE P49

HUMAN BODY QUIZ P44

1. a **2.** c **3.** b **4.** c **5.** b **6.** b **7.** a **8.** b **9.** a **10.** b

CLASSIFYING CREATURES P45

INVERTEBRATES: **octopus**
FISH: **shark**
BIRDS: **flamingo**
AMPHIBIANS: **toad**
MAMMALS: **monkey**
REPTILES: **gecko**

NIMAL DOT TO DOT P50

e dots reveal a **black rhinoceros**.

FOLLOW THE FUNCTION P52

ANIMAL CELLS

FAT CELL
The droplet of stored fat provides energy.
BONE-MAKING CELL
This cell's long strands help it to connect to other cells.
CILIATED CELL
The hair-like cilia waft particles away from airways.
SECRETORY CELL
Hormones are released by this cell.

PLANT CELLS

STARCH-STORING CELL
This cell stores energy-rich starch.
LEAF CELL
Green chloroplasts inside this cell make food
for the plant.
SUPPORTING CELL
This cell helps to support a plant's stem.
FRUIT CELL
This cell helps to make a plant's fruit juicy.

OUCH SECTIONS P51

CLOWNING AROUND P53

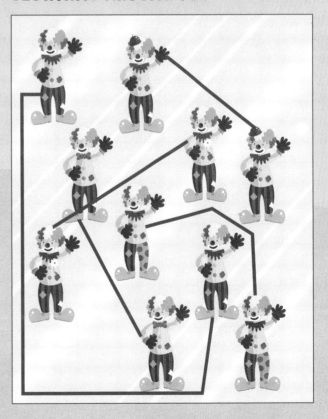

EARTH QUIZ P56

1. a **2.** c **3.** a **4.** c **5.** c **6.** a **7.** c **8.** b **9.** c **10.** a

FIND THE BATTERIES P57

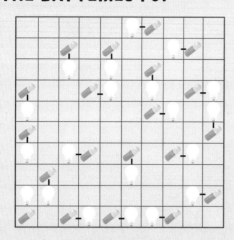

RUBBISH REMOVAL P58

There are: **7** aluminium cans, **8** yogurt pots,
7 plastic bottles, **5** cardboard boxes, **4** newspapers
and **5** glass bottles.

ROCKET PARTS P59

Group **B**

WORKBENCH JUMBLE P60

HOPSCOTCH SEQUENCES P61

A. 7, 14, 21, **28**, 35, **42**, 49
B. 1, **8**, 15, **22**, 29, 36, 43
C. **2**, 9, 16, 23, **30**, 37, 44
D. 3, 10, **17**, 24, **31**, **38**, 45

SOUND WAVES P62–63

CAR – 74
RECYCLING TRUCK – 90
HELICOPTER – 87
SHIP – 120
TRAIN – 100
AEROPLANE –130

LET'S ROCK P64

H,9, E,8, B,5, J,7, C,7, H,2, D,1, H,5

WHERE'S THE HARE? P65

LIGHTNING MAZE P66

OD ASTRONAUT OUT P67

PENGUIN STEPPING STONES P72

4, 8, 20, 36, 32, 48, 16, 12 and 28.

FINGERPRINT FINDING P73

Fingerprint **E** is the one that matches.

GLOW-STICK HUNT P74

There are: **8** blue wands, **9** orange sticks,
12 green sticks, **9** yellow stars,
5 yellow and pink wands and **2** blue glasses.

UNDERWATER JIGSAW P77

Pieces **D** and **E**

SOLAR-PANEL PUZZLE P78

The fourth house (with the purple garage door)
is having solar panels installed.

FOOD CHAINS P79

Seaweed, **fish**, **seal**, **shark**
Leaf, **earthworm**, chicken, **hawk**

ALANCE-POD PYRAMIDS P68

a. 130 b. 108   **3**. a. 125 b. 85 c. 55

a. 235 b. 155   **4**. a. 250 b. 130 c. 160

OTATING LOLLIES P69

oups **C** and **F** match each other.

ENE SPOTTING P70

RADIOACTIVE COUNTING P80

There are: **2** pink, **1** blue, **2** green, **3** yellow, **2** orange
and **2** red.

MARKET MUDDLE P81

LINDA: fruit and vegetables   DEV: fish
CLARA: bread   DALE: juice

YCLING CO-ORDINATES P71

For the zebra crossing   2. A toy shop
G,7   **4**. J,9   **5**. D,2 and F,7

SOLID, LIQUID OR GAS? P82

SOLID: wood, sand, ice
LIQUID: water, honey, milk
GAS: oxygen, helium, steam

MATCHING MAGNETS P83

ODD SOCKS P88

PERIODIC PUZZLE P84–85

1. Rubidium   3. Sulphur   5. Argon
2. Magnet   4. Mercury

SKI SEASON P89

A. Anya B. Sam C. Rhona

PLANTS QUIZ P86

1. b 2. c 3. c 4. a 5. a 6. b 7. c 8. b 9. c 10. b

PUMPING BALLOONS P90

Astrid has pumped the biggest balloon.

BAFFLING BRIDGES P87

DRONE CLOSE-UPS P91

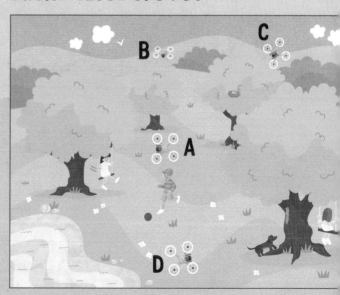

1. B   3. A
2. C   4. D

GGING FOR DINOSAURS P92–93

EED FOR SPEED P94

up **B** contains all of the parts.

LIMBING HIGH P95

e highest mountain is called **Mount Everest**.

ERTEBRATE VERSUS

NVERTEBRATE P96

g: 8, 2, 24, 12, 4

ail: 3, 29, 7, 25, 13

UNDER THREAT P97

The **tiger** and the **elephant** make it to the river.

MICRO-DOKU P98

1.

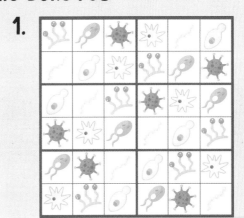

2.

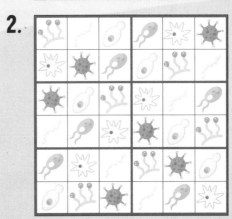

WAY OF THE WATER P99

H,6, B,7, H,2, G,8, C,9, G,4, I,3, B,4

DISCOVERY MIX-UP P100

Carl Wilhelm Scheele discovered oxygen in 1773. He used an instrument that heated a chemical mixture and collected the oxygen in a bladder tied to the end.

Andre Geim and Kostya Nosolev discovered graphine in 2004. It is only one atom thick, making it the thinnest known material.

Our prehistoric ancestors discovered fire around 1.5 million years ago. It became vital for heat, light and protection from predators.

Marie and Pierre Curie discovered the elements radium and polonium in 1898. Marie became the first woman to win a Nobel Prize.

In 1878, Hilaire de Chardonnet discovered that rayon can be used to make synthetic silk.

John Dalton was the first person to provide evidence for the existence of the atom, in 1803.

TINY TREES P101

A is the youngest tree.

WEIGHING PARCELS P102

A. 275g B. 400g C. 625g D. 175g

ERUPTING VOLCANOS P103

ROLLER-COASTER RIDE P104

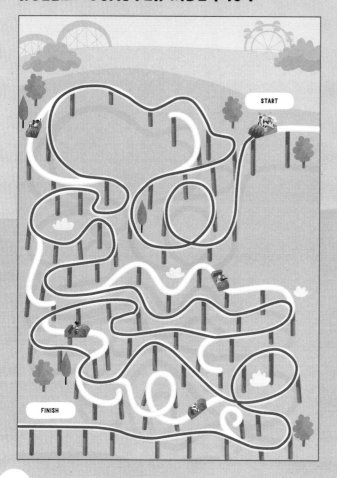

BALANCED DIET P105

Recipe card C uses all the ingredients.

MATCHING MINERALS P106

COUNTING POOS P107

There are 29 green bacteria.

CONGO COUNTING P108–109

There are: 2 gorillas, 3 leopards, 3 serpent eagles, 5 pangolins, 11 grey parrots and 3 okapis.

LLOYS BRAIN-TEASER P110

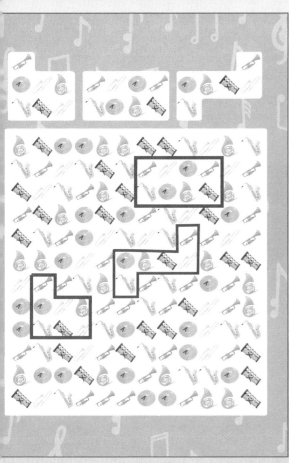

NIMALS: TRUE OR FALSE? P111

True
False (mammals such as dolphins live in water)
False (elephants grow in the womb for 22 months)
True
True
True
True
False (they use their tongues, not their noses)
True
False (fish have gills instead of lungs)

HEMICAL REACTIONS P112

BONE UP P113

Group **B** contains all of the bones.

DOTTY BODY PART P114

The body part is a **brain**.

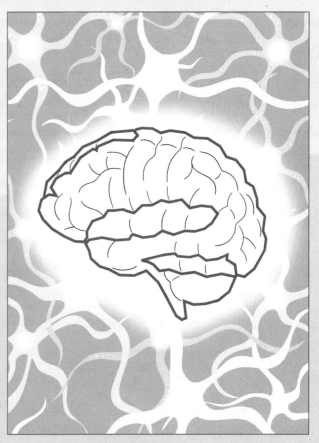

TUG OF WAR P115

Blue team: 5   Yellow team: 10
Green team: 11   Red team: 12
The red team wins.

GLOSSARY

Bacteria
These are tiny organisms found throughout nature (including in your own body). Some bacteria can make you ill, but other kinds are good for you.

Carbohydrates
Carbohydrates are compounds made of carbon, hydrogen and oxygen. Foods such as potatoes, bread and rice are high in carbohydrates.

Cardiac
This word is used to describe things that relate to the heart. A 'cardiac arrest', for example, is when the heart stops pumping blood around the body.

Cells
Cells are small structures that make up all plants and animals. There are many kinds of cells, all doing different jobs.

Chloroplasts
These are parts of certain plant cells. Chloroplasts turn sunlight into energy for plants, in a process called 'photosynthesis'.

Combustion
This is the scientific word for burning.

Density
If you divide an object or substance's mass by its volume, you get its density.

DNA
Short for deoxyribonucleic acid, DNA carries the instructions that tell all living things how to grow and function.

Ecosystem
An ecosystem is a natural area in which living things interact with and rely upon each other. Non-living things such as water and soil are also important parts of an ecosystem.

Element
An element is a substance that cannot be broken down into any other substance (oxygen and hydrogen, for example).

Hormones
Hormones are chemicals that help cells to do their jobs properly. Insulin, for example, is a hormone that controls the amount of sugar in your blood.

Nutrients
Living things need nutrients to stay healthy. Vitamins and fibre are examples of nutrients needed for a balanced diet.

Organisms
All living things are organisms.

Paleontologist
A paleontologist is a scientist who studies fossils in order to learn about prehistoric life.

Periodic table
This is a chart listing every known element.

Preservative
A preservative is a chemical that can be added to food so that it lasts longer.

Radioactive
When an unstable element breaks down it can become radioactive, causing it to emit energy known as radiation. Radiation can be very harmful to people.

Sterilize
If you sterilize something, you make it completely clean and free from germs.

Thermometer
A device used for measuring temperature.

Turbine
A machine that uses air, gas or water to turn a wheel, which then generates power.